Thomas Thomas of Pontypool

Radical Puritan

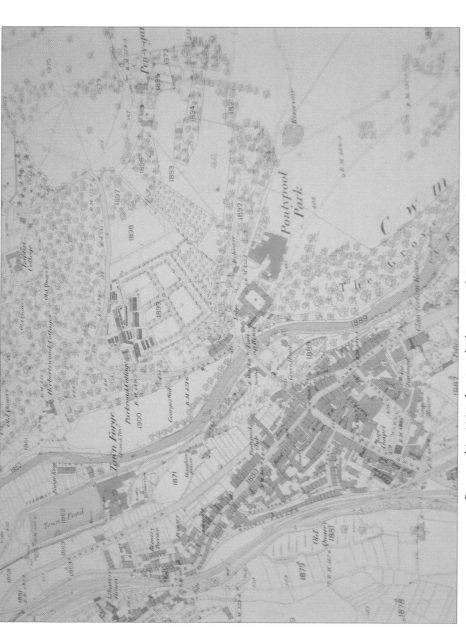

Pontypool in 1881 showing the locations of Crane Street and Penygarn
(Courtesy, Gwent Record Office, Cwmbran)

THOMAS THOMAS OF PONTYPOOL

Radical Puritan

A Biography

Arthur J. Edwards

APECS Press
Caerleon

First published in 2009 by APECS Press

*Editing and design by
APECS Press Caerleon*

The publisher acknowledges the financial support
of the Welsh Books Council and the
Isla Johnston Trust of the Church in Wales

ISBN 978 0 9548940 4 7 (Hardback)
978 0 9548940 8 5 (Paperback)

Printed in Wales by
Dinefwr Press, Llandybïe, Carmarthenshire, SA18 3YD

In memory of my parents,
Doris and Will Edwards

Contents

❦

Part Four: The Wisdom of Age, 1870-1881

Part Five: Epilogue

Appendix

Foreword

WHEN, in 1836, Thomas Thomas accepted an invitation to preside at the newly relocated Baptist Academy and to pastor a new English Baptist church in Pontypool, the church itself had not actually been formed, and the Academy had no building. In spite of this, he laboured successfully in Pontypool for forty years and on his retirement he handed to his successors a thriving church and a flourishing academy.

Born in Cowbridge, Thomas Thomas's family had moved to farm in the Cardiff area. As a lad he had joined a company of Welsh Baptists which formed itself into Tabernacle Baptist Church, Cardiff, in 1821. At the early age of 16, he began preaching and was admitted into the Abergavenny Academy the following year, moving on in 1824 to the Stepney Academy in London. There he spent a further four years as a student before being ordained the minister of Henrietta Street Baptist church in 1828. It was from that flourishing church in London that he returned to the uncertainty of Pontypool.

Thomas Thomas was an ardent dissenter, a zealous social reformer and a passionate supporter of education for the masses. He combined the role of an educator with that of an evangelist. An inspiring teacher, he was also an able organiser who supported the causes affecting the community. Many of the battles he fought were against the role and the authority of the State church; and it is therefore pleasing that an Anglican clergyman and historian has taken an interest in Thomas's life and penned an evaluation of his contribution.

Canon Arthur Edwards has examined the life and work of Thomas Thomas in detail and in this study he makes observations and shares insights that are all the more valuable since they are written by an Anglican scholar. This biography is based upon much original research by Canon Edwards. The family letters in the archive boxes of Thomas H. Thomas, their youngest son, add considerably to our understanding of the personal relationships of Thomas and Mary Thomas with their close family and the wider family of students and church members.

With his warm and friendly links with the leaders of the State church in the nineteenth century, Thomas Thomas would have been pleased to learn that one day a biography of a Nonconformist pastor would be written by the Senior Canon of the Diocese of Monmouth in the Church in Wales. That in itself reflects Thomas's far-sighted awareness of the value of cooperation between religious leaders in bringing about greater understanding and improved social development.

Cardiff
March 2009

D. Hugh Matthews
Former Principal
South Wales Baptist College
Cardiff, 1991-2001

Acknowledgements

T HIS biography began at the stimulus of the Revd D. Hugh Matthews, who invited me in 1993, when he was Principal of the South Wales Baptist College, to give a lecture on Dr Thomas Thomas of Pontypool. This lecture marked the centenary of the transfer of the Baptist College from Pontypool to Cardiff and was given in the hall of Trevethin Comprehensive School, once the home of Pontypool Baptist College. I am very grateful to my friends Hugh and Verina Matthews who encouraged me to write this biography and made it more accessible to the general reader by their helpful criticisms of the manuscript.

Other friends at that lecture in 1993 also encouraged publication. I am sorry that they have had to wait so long for this biography, which has been set aside many times in the course of a busy ministry. I am grateful to Mrs Jeanette Williams Secretary of Caerleon Endowed Junior School for typing the manuscript. It owes its publication now to the interest and zeal of its publishers Alun and Margaret Isaac of APECS Press Caerleon.

The unsung heroes and heroines of all such works as this are the librarians of the institutions that keep the records. I recall with pleasure the patience and assistance of the Librarian/Archivist of Regent's Park College, Oxford, the Librarian and staff of the National Library of Wales, Aberystwyth, the Librarians and staff of the Reference Libraries at Cardiff, Newport and Swansea and the County Archivists and staff of the Record Offices of Gwent and South Glamorgan. My debt to them is clear from the many primary and secondary sources that are quoted in the Select Bibliography.

My greatest debt is to Christine, my wife, who has not only taught students in Pontypool with as much distinction and for almost as long as Thomas did, but has even had to put up with more of Pontypool when at home.

Preface

TWENTY-TWO years ago in the preface to my biography of Archbishop Charles Green, I suggested that there were three reasons to justify its publication. Apart from the intrinsic merits of the Archbishop's life and works, the biography was intended to deepen our understanding of the arguments in the disestablishment campaign, and to widen our understanding of the history of those communities where the he had lived and worked.

Those reasons apply equally to this biography of Dr Thomas Thomas, a great Baptist Radical who might seem at first to be a very different religious leader from Dr Green, a distinguished Anglican Conservative. The two men represent both sides of the campaign for the Disestablishment of the Church in Wales. You cannot have the one without the other. You cannot understand the campaign for Church Defence under Charles Green without recognising the force of the arguments for disestablishment and the deep conviction with which they were held by such an intelligent Welsh religious leader as Thomas Thomas.

Such a leader deserves a biography, not simply because he became the first Welsh-speaking Welshman to become the President of the Baptist Union of Great Britain and Ireland, but also because he was a pioneer in so many enterprises during the course of a distinguished career.

He was the first minister of an English Baptist church in Pontypool. He was the first President of the Baptist College in Pontypool. He was the first President of the Monmouthshire English Baptist Association. He gave early prominence in Monmouthshire to the movement for adult suffrage because he believed that the success of the Anti-Corn Law League, which he supported, depended upon the achievement of parliamentary representation. He was the first person to propose a Church Rate abolition society in Pontypool. He spearheaded a branch of the Liberation Society in Pontypool as well as the cause of Temperance throughout South Wales.

Thomas Thomas has long been a neglected leader in South Wales. This is partly because he spent most of his life in nineteenth century Monmouthshire. The Anglican Church in the county was part of the Diocese of Llandaff and Welsh historians have given much more attention to Glamorgan in their studies of the period. Their assumptions about the importance of the Welsh language in the lives of industrial migrant workers do not hold true for Monmouthshire, as Thomas realised. More than that, the greatest of our Welsh historians have misunderstood him even when they have heard of him. This biography is an attempt to redress the balance for Thomas, for Monmouthshire and for Pontypool, its oldest industrial town and one that is still without a publication of its proper history.

The significance of this biography for our understanding of the spiritual and religious history of the whole Church in Wales lies in the relationships that are revealed in the extended community over time, through the co-operation and interplay of religious leaders and institutions for the well-being of society. The leaders of those times were united by their common concerns until their integrity and good-will were challenged by the restraints of an Established Church. Such evidence of co-operation should be an encourage-ment for closer ecumenical participation in a disestablished Church today.

Caerleon, Newport   Arthur J. Edwards
April 2009

Part One

FORMATIVE YEARS

One

From Birth to Baptism, London and Wales

THOMAS Thomas was born at Cowbridge in the Vale of Glamorgan on 12 January 1805 and baptised in the local parish church on 28 March. The baptism register provides the only record of his birth since there was no civil registration at that time. He was named Thomas after his father, a farmer whose physical features the son inherited, but with whom he later came to have little else in common. His mother, Mary, showed sympathy with his spiritual awakening as a teenager and his later vocation to the Baptist Ministry and she won over his reluctant father to their son's side. Yet the formation of Thomas's Christian faith was not owed to the influence of his home.

Very soon after Thomas Thomas was baptised, the family moved to a small farm at Leckwith Bridge near Cardiff. Here, Thomas spent an uneventful childhood in a home where he learned to speak both Welsh and English and to read them both at the local Sunday school. He was a healthy child and his only misfortune was to be kicked on the ear at the age of seven by the hoof of a runaway mare, to which he attributed his deafness in later life. Between the ages of eight and ten, Thomas received his elementary education from the Revd Thomas Lewis at Llandaff. To this tuition at the hands of a clergyman of the Established Church, Thomas later attributed both his clear, bold handwriting and his musical ability.

By early adolescence Thomas became very conscious of God's presence in his life. He used afterwards to describe how he had prayed earnestly in the farm meadow and had talked about religious matters with two of the farm labourers who took him to their Chapel services in Cardiff. Thomas listened to the sermons of the Revd Griffith Davies who became the first Minister of Tabernacle Baptist Church and prepared Thomas for his baptism by immersion in the River Taff. On the day arranged for the baptism Thomas's mother went with him to the River Taff in Cardiff, where Thomas was forcibly taken home by his father before the baptism could take place. Thomas's father objected to his son's second baptism. He was himself a member of the Church of England and Thomas later told his own children that his father occasionally attended services in Llandaff Cathedral; his opposition to his son's baptism was expressed more with the logic of a farmer than a theologian, that he had paid the Vicar of Cowbridge once for his son's baptism and he did not see any reason to repeat it.

It was Mary Thomas who successfully pleaded with her husband to let the baptism in the Taff go ahead at the second attempt on 22 November 1818, a date that was so important to Thomas, now aged 13, that it remained indelibly impressed on his mind. From that time Thomas's education was entirely in the hands of the Revd William Jones, a young Baptist Minister of twenty-eight who had opened a school as part of his ministry at Bethany Church in Cardiff. Jones was impressed with Thomas's ability and he made him an usher in his school. At such an impressionable age, Thomas was deeply influenced by Jones and for ever indebted to him.

Under the influence of William Jones, Thomas preached his first sermon at Tabernacle Chapel in 1821 at the age of sixteen after much previous experience of speaking at nearby cottage and farm-house meetings.

In 1875, when Thomas published his *Memoirs of the Life and Labours of the Revd Thomas Jones of Chepstow*, he recalled the harsh and unreceptive conditions under which he and Jones, his fellow-labourer, had preached the Gospel in the Vale of Glamorgan more than fifty years earlier.

Revd Micah Thomas, 1778-1853.
Tutor, Abergavenny Baptist Academy
(Courtesy, South Wales Baptist College, Cardiff)

Through the Christian fellowship at Tabernacle Thomas experienced his vocation to the ministry and he applied to enter the Baptist Academy at Abergavenny. His father had further objections to this move but his mother came once more to his rescue. She provided clothes and transport so that the Revd Micah Thomas, the tutor there, was able to record in his diary that Thomas Thomas entered the academy to train for the Baptist Ministry on 2 September 1822. Abergavenny was a very small academy and Micah Thomas its only tutor. It had been established since 1807 primarily to teach English to young Welsh preachers.

Thomas Thomas understood Welsh better than English at that time, though his English was better than the other eight students. At Abergavenny, he learnt Latin and Greek so that he could read the New Testament in its original language, a practice he continued for the rest of his life. He also used the opportunities to preach in local churches on Sundays.

On 23 August 1824, Thomas transferred to Stepney College, London, later Regent's Park College. Dr Murch was its President and Thomas learned Hebrew as well as advancing in Greek and Theology. He worked hard and was highly regarded as a local preacher. As a result he was called to minister at Henrietta Street Church in Brunswick Square, where he was ordained at the age of 21, on 18 July 1828.

On holidays from Stepney College Thomas had spent most time at the home of Mary David, the beautiful second daughter of Llewellyn and Joan David who lived near Cardiff Castle. They long planned to get married and this took place within two years of Thomas's ordination. They were married in St John's Church in Cardiff by licence on 22 February 1830. Both bride and groom

'Aenon', Micah Thomas's home and the site of the Abergavenny Baptist Academy
(Courtesy, South Wales Baptist College, Cardiff)

were Baptists and among the wedding guests were the Revd William Jones of Bethany Chapel as well as the great Baptist minister, Christmas Evans. However, when Thomas Thomas, bachelor of the parish of St Pancras, married Mary David, a spinster of the parish of St Mary's, Cardiff, only the curate of St John's Church was allowed to officiate. So Thomas and Mary were married like every other couple at that time according to the rites and ceremonies of the Church of England and only an ordained minister of the Church of England was allowed to officiate at the ceremony.

Such were the disabilities of Nonconformists in those days. They could not be married in their own Churches nor buried in parish Churchyards by their own rites; neither could they take degrees at English universities. It was Thomas's fate to have been born too early to take advantage of the removal of these disabilities and that contributed to his determination to work for their removal. Within seven years of his marriage at St John's Church Nonconformists could get married in their own chapels.

In an even shorter time Thomas could have registered for a degree at the new University College London in Gower Street, within walking distance of his Chapel at Henrietta Street. By that time, Thomas had moved to Pontypool, and so he remained among the countless intelligent people who were never able to take a degree. His doctorate was honorary, conferred at a later date by the American University of Indiana.

After their marriage, Thomas and Mary returned to Henrietta Street where the happiness and confidence that he gained from his marriage soon enriched his energetic and successful ministry. Thomas preached in the open air as well as in the Chapel. He lectured on the New Testament and developed the pastoral care that was offered by the Chapel. On 18 September 1831, Mary Thomas gave birth to their first son, named Llewellyn after her father. It was a Sunday and Thomas preached three times at his Chapel as usual.

The first publication that has survived from Thomas's pen is the Pastoral Letter that he issued to Henrietta Street Chapel on 25

November 1835 after being the minister there for seven years. Thomas had always been serious, even as a child, and he took his pastoral responsibility very seriously. He regarded every Nonconformist minister as a bishop (overseer) in his own right. Thomas's letter, with its seven simple directives for the pastoral care of his flock, reveals a mature understanding of what should characterise a church that is well-governed in the light of the Gospel. Like all such letters, it reveals as much about the writer as it does about the recipients.

Thomas stated that they should behave as Christians with consistency and propriety; sincerity and benevolence; virtuous manners and wise conversation. They should cultivate brotherly love and discourage gossip. Concern for the welfare of their fellow-members should be a hall-mark of their Church membership. As the members increased rapidly under Thomas's leadership, there was an increased need for the deacons of the Church to supervise the pastoral care that was provided by all the members for one another. Only if all matters were communicated to the deacons, could Thomas know all the circumstances of individual hardship.

Thomas encouraged his members to do more private reading, meditation and prayer and to organise family prayers. They should be "regular, punctual and constant" in their own attendance at Church; they should not simply be concerned about their own spiritual welfare but should show "affectionate solicitude" for the spiritual growth of their fellow members.

Thomas's description of himself as "your brother and overseer," illustrates the way he regarded himself as a bishop of a gathered congregation that was well organised on fairly strict Calvinist lines. He made it clear that membership of the Church should be limited to those who were renewed and sanctified by the Gospel, because, "an unrenewed and unsanctified member" would be "simulating what he does not feel and professing what he does not possess." Such a member would end up feeling very guilty and would be exposed to "proportionate wrath" from God. So for the sake of the souls of unbelievers, it would be better not to place them in situations where they would have to pretend to be believers.

Thomas's pastoral letter was a clear, sensitive and sensible Christian document. It was addressed to a growing church in the heart of the city where it was clearly important to establish both his own relationship with all the members, and their relationships in love with one another, as well as their concern for material and spiritual care. He had also to establish some guidelines for evangelism and the relationships between the members of the Church and the casual attenders at church services. It was an impressive effort for a thirty-year-old minister in his first charge.

Two

Early Days in Pontypool

IN 1836, Thomas Thomas was invited to become the first President of the Baptist College that was about to be transferred to Pontypool from Abergavenny, where it had been based since 1807 under its only tutor, Micah Thomas. During that time the population of Pontypool had increased seven-fold from the couple of thousand mainly Welsh people who lived there at the beginning of the century, and the number of Welsh-speakers had reduced to fifty-two per cent of the population. Yet Pontypool was an old industrial town, well-placed to occupy an important place in the industrial revolution. The local hills abounded in iron-ore and coal and there were furnaces and forges and tin-works in the neighbourhood. Even before 'coal was king', Pontypool had become an important railway junction with three stations by 1860. Capel Hanbury Leigh, heir to a long line of Hanburys at Park House, had injected new life into the Pontypool Iron Works.

By 1836, Pontypool was a large town by Welsh standards. It lay in the parish of Trevethin, but the parish Church, on a hill outside the town, was served only by a curate of the rural parish of Llanover. All the major religious denominations had built their places of worship in the town, but Pontypool was unique in having a small church, dedicated to St James, that had been built for the provision of worship solely in the English language. This indicated the origins of many of the industrial workers as well as the shopkeepers of the town. It was nevertheless a bilingual town and shop assistants had to be able to speak both Welsh and English.

Pontypool was well-placed to become the headquarters of the Baptists in south-east Wales. The leadership of the local Baptists was

Present day view of St James's Church, built in 1821 for the benefit of English-speaking people in Pontypool, unable to understand Welsh. Note, the Town Hall in the background built by the Lord Lieutenant, Capel Hanbury Leigh to celebrate the birth of his son and heir in 1853

concentrated in the hands of a few families whose fortunes had grown through intermarriage with those in the forefront of the developing local industries. Micah Thomas, the tutor of the Abergavenny Academy, was himself part of that extended family of Baptist leaders which had originated with Miles Harry, the remarkable Baptist evangelist of the eighteenth century. Harry had been the pastor at Penygarn Baptist Chapel and he was one of the five masters at the first Baptist academy in Wales at Trosnant, Pontypool, in 1732. Another master was John Griffiths, a learned layman and acting manager of the Pontypool Iron and Japan works, where the first English Baptist Church originated in the nineteenth century. Miles Harry's nephew, Morgan, was the father of John Harris of Govilon, a prominent Baptist layman whose two daughters, Mary Anne and Rachel, married respectively John Conway, tinworks proprietor and founder of Pontrhydyrun Baptist Church, and Micah Thomas, the Baptist minister and tutor of Abergavenny. Conway's daughter, Ann, married David Evans, the Baptist minister of Pontrhydyrun.

The Phillips family of Pontypool was also part of this Baptist clan by direct descent from Pastor Miles Harry through his son Henry and his grand-daughter Ann. Edward Harris Phillips, a local surgeon and deputy lieutenant of the county, was a great-grandson of Miles Harry as was his brother, William of Maesderwen, squire Hanbury's agent and long-serving treasurer of the Baptist College. William Phillips was a pillar of Crane Street Baptist Chapel and a very good friend to Thomas Thomas. Phillips and Conway and Micah Thomas were all related by marriage.

The School of the Prophets at Trosnant, Pontypool, which Miles Harry had helped to found in 1732, came to an end in 1770. From that date until Micah Thomas started his Academy at Abergavenny in 1807, the Baptist ministers of Wales depended upon Bristol Baptist College for their training. Micah Thomas was primarily concerned to prepare young Welsh ministers to preach effectively in the English language. Thomas Thomas had been one of his most able students and Thomas inherited his mantle and much of his theological and political outlook, which he passed on to his successor William Edwards more than forty years later.

It was essential that young Baptist ministers in South-east Wales should be able to preach effectively in English. This became more true as the nineteenth century progressed and the Baptists were the first to realise that successful evangelism depended upon good communication in English. For this, Micah Thomas and Thomas Thomas were in turn criticised by Welsh zealots in their denomination. They were also criticised for seeming to sit lightly to the harsh tenets of high Calvinism and were accused of being tainted with the Arminianism of Anglicanism.

When Micah Thomas had been head of the Baptist College at Abergavenny, he had been involved in much controversy because he held a more liberal view of atonement through Jesus Christ than most Baptists who then believed with John Calvin that Jesus died for certain particular people and not for the whole world. His view was close to that of Andrew Fuller, an earlier Baptist Minister. Most

Anglicans then believed that the work of salvation brought about by Jesus Christ was for all people. This view was shared by Wesleyan Methodists. The conflict between Calvinists and Arminians or Fullerites was strong in South Wales in the 1820s and Micah Thomas was blamed for much of it. He was accused of favouring students in the College who shared his views and even of reading John Wesley's works at the breakfast table.

Both Micah Thomas and Thomas Thomas shared a radical political outlook that supported liberal causes and they were especially concerned about the disabilities of Nonconformists in relation to the Established Church of England. Micah Thomas had successfully proposed the deferment of a Church Rate in the parish vestry meeting at Abergavenny and his example was not wasted on his successor at a later date.

The Church Rate was a tax for the repair of the buildings and support of the worship of the Established Church of England. It was levied upon everyone who lived in the parish and it was a major grievance for Nonconformists because they had to pay for the upkeep of something to which they did not belong. Compulsory Church Rate was eventually abolished by Gladstone in 1868 but it had been very difficult to collect before that time because it had to be agreed at the annual Vestry Meeting of the parish at which all electors (including Nonconformists) could vote. Micah Thomas secured the postponement of the church Rate in Abergavenny in 1836 and Thomas Thomas proposed the formation of the Pontypool Church Rate Abolition Society in 1837.

Micah Thomas and his circle had long considered moving the one-tutor academy from Abergavenny to Pontypool to place it at the centre of the county and in the midst of an expanding industrial town that would afford easy access to the most flourishing Baptist churches in the area. With the growth of local industries and the leadership of Baptist industrialists, there was every possibility that the proposed new English Baptist Church at Pontypool would provide the financial support needed by the new College Principal to sustain him in his work.

Pontypool Baptist College, Penygarn, 1836-1893

Even Crane Street, in all her future glory, was not arrayed like Henrietta Street Chapel in prospects and pay for a young Baptist minister in 1836, but Thomas Thomas was Welsh and his loyalties led him to accept the joint post at Pontypool. He and his wife, Mary, and their infant sons, Llewellyn and William, moved to Pontypool in the summer of 1836. For the time being he and his family and the college had to make do with temporary accommodation on an annual salary of £140. The English Chapel would follow later. There were seven students in training for the ministry, five of them transferred from Abergavenny and most of them were older than Thomas himself. He had to teach them everything from Hebrew to English as well as the art of preaching. William Phillips, Treasurer of the Baptist College organised the finances and presided at the meetings of the College Council.

The foundation stone of the new college at Penygarn was laid by Thomas's son Llewellyn on 3 August 1836. The impressive new building, supervised by Robert Carter of Pontypool, who also built the workhouse, was completed in one year at a cost of £1,840. It had to be enlarged more than once in the next twenty years, but it was always Thomas's job to help raise the money for the college building, by hard campaigning in Baptist Churches throughout South Wales.

The College overlooked the smoke-filled town of Pontypool. The conditions of life and labour for the industrial workers were harsh and the totem of this unjust hardship was the workhouse at nearby Coed-y-Gric, opened a year after the College. The workhouse was feared more in prospect than reality as a symbol of cruel oppression and deprivation by far more people than ever darkened its doors. Although the number of inmates at Coed-y-Gric was only 101 by 1851, the workhouse was a powerful focus of political discontent after the failure of the Reform Act of 1832 to do anything to improve the parliamentary representation of the townspeople of Pontypool. Before the Reform Act, Capel Hanbury Leigh had received threatening letters and had his property set on fire, but after the Act the town of Pontypool, together with Abergavenny and Caerleon, remained without an MP while Monmouth, Usk and Newport with smaller populations were represented in parliament by Reginald Blewitt of Llantarnam. To modern minds, unfamiliar with working-class life in Britain in the decade or so after 1815, it might seem strange that people placed so much hope in the possible improvement of the quality of that life by increasing their right to be represented in parliament.

Support for the Reform movement that produced the Reform Act of 1832 was given for just such a purpose. Working people found it impossible to improve either their wages or their working conditions, when combinations of workers for such purposes were first proscribed and then prevented from exerting pressure. Had the Reform Act given better representation in parliament, it would still have been many years before the poor could hope for better conditions of work. As it happened, the Reform Act benefited only middle class voters and left the working class unenfranchised. The threat of poverty and unemployment was intensified by the abolition of the parish control of financial relief for the poor that had been in place for centuries. The relief for able-bodied poor after 1834 was only available in the union workhouse and this formed the background of fear against which Chartism was formed.

Chartism was the movement that developed in the late 1830's to achieve the six points of the People's Charter. The Charter was published in 1838 by the London Working Men's Association set up two years earlier. The aims of the Charter were universal manhood suffrage (a vote for every man over the age of twenty-one), a secret ballot, the abolition of the property qualifications for MPs, payment of MPs, constituencies of equal size and annual parliaments. The last aim was never achieved because it would have meant a general election every year!

There were important differences among the Chartist leaders about the tactics to be used to achieve the aims of the Charter. The two main groups have been designated Physical force and Moral force Chartists by historians. The former believed that change could only be achieved by armed violence while the latter believed only in non-violent protest and powerful persuasion such as petitioning Parliament and educating the workers in the aims of the Charter. It was protested by some that violent rhetoric in the cause of moral argument produced physical force, but the matter was never really as clear-cut in the minds of many Chartists as it seemed subsequently in the analysis of historians.

Like the whole Chartist movement, the Newport Rising could not have happened without the leadership of disaffected middle class leaders drawn from the ranks of tradespeople and shopkeepers, especially John Frost, a Newport draper and former Mayor of Newport, Zephaniah Williams, a publican from yeoman-farming stock and William Lloyd Jones, a watchmaker and beer-house keeper who came from a family of Bristol tradesmen.

The late David Jones described it as the Last Rising. He went further than anyone else to characterise it as an armed uprising. This challenged the claim, as John Frost said in his defence at Monmouth, that it was intended as nothing more than a monster demonstration.

John Frost

Zephaniah Williams

William Jones

Chartist leaders of the Newport Rising of 3-4 November, 1839

Some of the participants who marched in that three-pronged attack from Blackwood under John Frost, from Ebbw Vale under Zephaniah Williams and from Pontypool under William Jones on that fateful night of 3-4 November 1839, thought that they were taking part in an armed uprising to capture Newport and release Henry Vincent, the London Chartist, from prison in Monmouth. This would have meant a massive march of many hours on rocky roads. As it was, communications between the marchers at all stages was pathetically poor and the eastern valley Chartists failed to arrive on Stow Hill, Newport, before the riot outside the Westgate Hotel had been subdued by the soldiers.

The Working Men's Association at Pontypool was founded as early as 1838 and there were four Chartist lodges in the district. Prominent Pontypool radicals were on hand to become the captains of the Newport Rising in November 1839. These included John Llewellyn, a trade-unionist, beer-house keeper and a hatter (hat maker) of Pontnewynydd; he was treasurer of his local lodge. Also at Pontnewynydd as a shoemaker, as well as in George Street, Pontypool, was William Shellard, whose children, like those of John Britton, another Chartist, were baptised at Trevethin Church.

Solomon Britton, John's brother, was a brigade commander in the Newport Rising. He it was who led those wise men from the east who arrived in Newport too late for the fighting at the Westgate. The brigade under William Jones was certainly involved in the fighting and George Shell, whose father had founded the Pontypool Lodge, was killed. Others who were active members of the Pontypool Lodge included Evan Emanuel, a local turner, and Thomas Parry, secretary of the Lodge and a local shoemaker. Capel Hanbury Leigh complained that his iron miners had been forced to join the Chartist lodges. It is clear that the leadership of those lodges was provided by small tradesmen and shopkeepers.

The demands of the Charter made sense to a community that realised that unless Members of Parliament could be paid a salary, only Liberals of independent means, like the Hanburys and Reginald Blewitt could go to Westminster. Without the secret ballot, the vote was useless to industrial workers whose employment bound them to the will of the ironmasters. What hope was there for an iron miner when the curate of St Woolos' Church in Newport was sacked by the Vicar over a political disagreement in 1831? (*Monmouthshire Merlin*, 1 Oct. 1831). Ironically, eight years later, the Churchyard at St Woolos became the burial place of the Chartists who were killed outside the Westgate Hotel on the fourth of November.

None of this was lost on Thomas Thomas as he settled down in Pontypool. Nor could it be. The Chartist Rising was the most important event in the history of Monmouthshire in the first half of the nineteenth century.

The character of Pontypool is discerned and delineated by the descriptions and reports that subsequently analysed and agonised over the educational and social shortcomings of the society that had spawned the sedition.

The late David Jones in his book, *The Last Rising*, concluded that, "the message in the months after the Rising was 'enquire and secure'." The government did not conduct a full parliamentary inquiry into the Rising but Seymour Tremenheere, Inspector of Schools, was ordered to inspect the educational provisions of the area, including the Sunday Schools, and to report to the Lords of the Council how the activities of the Chartists had been kept unknown from the magistrates. Tremenheere's report was published in 1840. In the same year G. S. Kenrick, one of the proprietors of the Varteg Hill Iron Works in the Parish of Trevethin, published the first investigation by a local resident. The national press produced their own reports and the local authorities agonised over the causes of the Rising. There followed the infamous *Reports of the Commissioners of Inquiry into the state of education in Wales* in 1847, referred to later.

The results of the Rising upon local lives were out of all proportion to its failure. One less tangible result was its influence upon the minds of religious and social leaders at the time. Many of those leaders were men of liberal sympathies. They were concerned about the conditions in which the industrial workers lived as well as with the dangerous and unpredictable communities brought into being by social deprivation. It is understandable that they were frightened by the Newport Rising and gave greater prominence to the matter of law and order.

Three

The Chartist Sermon

IN November 1839, Thomas Thomas delivered a sermon at the Upper Trosnant Baptist Chapel on the subject of the Chartist Rising or "the civil duties of Christians" as "occasioned by the late outrages at Newport." The sermon was published in London just before the Revd Thomas Morris, his Welsh-Baptist counterpart in Tabernacle Chapel, Crane Street, had a sermon in Welsh on the same subject published in Cardiff. Both preachers condemned the method of physical force used by the Newport Chartists to achieve their aims, and they were both eager to assure their audiences that Nonconformists were loyal citizens of the state and in no way condoned violence. Thomas pointed out that the "principles of civil and religious liberty" maintained by the Nonconformists in no way supported the rising. On the contrary, Nonconformists had "deterred many thousands in the County of Monmouth from any participation in the Riots."

Thomas shared with other religious leaders a deep distrust of the consequences of physical violence. But he had more sympathy with the demands of the Charter and with the condition of the poor than his fellow-Baptist Thomas Morris or the Rector of Dowlais, Evan Davies, who also published a sermon on the subject. Thomas had a social conscience and a deep resentment of the imposition of the Church Rate upon Nonconformists as well as their civil disabilities, but their grievances did not make them disloyal subjects of the queen or enemies of liberty. The stance that Thomas advocated in his sermon towards civil injustice was that of "passive submission" as advocated by George Fox, the leader of the Quakers.

Like other Nonconformists, Thomas was clearly stung by the attempts of some journalists to lay blame for the rising upon the "principles of civil and religious liberty" maintained by the Nonconformists. Thomas asserted that Nonconformists had always held an "ardent attachment to the civil constitution of the realm." The assertion of this loyalty became a matter of principle for many Nonconformists and almost a guarantee of their respectability. It had an echoing chord in the comment appended to the return made by the Independent Chapel at New Inn, Pontypool, in response to the Religious Census of 1851: "God save the Queen: no popery!" Papists might seek by their foreign allegiance to subvert the constitution, but puritans were loyal subjects! Nonconformists did not want to be easy scapegoats for the deep political anxiety aroused in respectable society by the physical force methods of the Chartists.

It is not therefore surprising that Thomas overstated his case by claiming that there were not fifty dissenters among the Chartist marchers and tried to have his cake and eat it by showing in an appendix to his sermon how many more people in the parish of Trevethin had been nurtured and educated by the English and Welsh chapels and schools of the Nonconformists than had been achieved by the Established Church. He then threw back in the teeth of the establishment its claim that everyone who did not attend a Nonconformist Chapel was a "*bona fide* member of the National Church," and therefore the majority of the Chartist marchers must have been members of the Church of England.

The text of Thomas's sermon was Matthew 22, Verse 21, "Render therefore unto Caesar the things which are Caesar's; and unto God the things that are God's." He urged upon his hearers a "general obedience to all civil laws under every form of government"; he quoted both the teaching of St Paul in Romans, Chapter 13 and that of Chapter 2 of the First Epistle of St Peter, in defence of this general duty of submission. He went on to ask what the just limitations of such civil obedience might be, and he quoted the conduct of Paul and Silas in Acts 16, and Paul's response to the illegal behaviour of Ananias in Acts 22, to conclude that "it cannot be a man's duty to do what, in his conscience, he believes to be a sin against God whose authority is paramount to every other . . . we are indeed bound to render to Caesar the things which are Caesar's, but we are equally bound not to render to Caesar the things which are God's." The examples of Jesus, Daniel and the Prophets, as well as the boldness of Peter and John in Acts 4 and 5, corroborate this principle.

We should pay to Caesar our lawful taxes to support the "legitimate objects of civil government," said Thomas, "but we are not obliged to pay illegal taxes or what is demanded for objects that lie beyond the province of the civil ruler such as religious purposes." The example of the Quakers and others who have "patiently and from year to year, suffered 'the spoiling of their goods' and, in some instances, the loss of liberty and life, rather than pay legal exactions for the support of what is contrary to God's will," was praised by Thomas. He challenged the right of the State to impose a religion upon the people and he denied the right of that State-imposed religion to use the taxes levied by the State for religious purposes, because our consciences and forms of worship belong to God.

At the same time, Thomas thought that the magistrate should be respected for his office, regardless of his personal character, and we should pray for our rulers, as Paul urged Timothy (1 Tim. 2: 1-2). The existing authorities provided us with settled government, security, liberty, law and peace. Without the rule of law there would be anarchy and revolution and, "what was seen and felt on the memorable night of the third of November 1839, was but a faint representation in miniature of what would occur, were the whole constitution and government of the country entirely destroyed; and the kingdom abandoned to the fury of a lawless population, urged on to cruel excesses by restless spirits who make the profession of liberty, a cloak of political licentiousness, because bloody revolutions, effected by physical force, may be expected to give birth to new evils as formidable as those they were designed to abolish." The government could command stronger forces than the protesters and could inflict worse penalties.

Thomas believed that much more could have been achieved by, "oft-repeated appeals to the reason and conscience of the legislature and the nation; by unceasing efforts to enlist the sympathies of the population in the cause of the oppressed; and especially by a *passive* obedience to bad laws, and moral resistance to the encroachment of unconstitutional power." He cited the examples of the Quakers and the Churchwardens of Llanelly and Llanon who had been imprisoned for resisting Church Rate in 1837 as had Thoroughgood, the Chelmsford cobbler in 1839.

In his sermon, Thomas clearly distanced himself and all dissenters from the physical resistance to lawful authority he judged to be criminal and unwise. It is impossible to be precise about the number of Pontypool people involved in the Chartist march on Newport on that fateful night of 3-4 November 1839; it is unlikely that many of them, if any, heard Thomas's sermon, though some of his hearers would have been Chartist sympathisers. Thomas was painting on a wider canvas and presenting a clear picture of his own future pattern of activity. Some of his listeners may well have wondered why he had not spoken out sooner about the threat posed by physical force Chartism instead of seeming to be wise after the event. To that he gave a clear answer at the end of his sermon: "I did not at all participate in the alarm which great numbers expressed in these parts, as I felt no doubt that the very extravagance and violence of the demagogues would soon work their own cure, and persuaded myself that the sound sense of the common people would prove sufficient antidote to the poison of their physical-force doctrine."

Thomas expressed the hope that the government would exercise a more liberal and vigorous policy to remove the grievances and concede the rights of the poorer classes. To that extent, Thomas's sermon could only have helped the poor.

The sermon identified Thomas as a successor to the Quaker, George Fox in his advocacy of passive resistance. What brought the sermon into the arena of public debate was not its unobjectionable contents but the Appendix that accompanied its publication. The sermon thus joins that large number of publications whose significance lies largely in the controversy that surrounded their publication.

In the case of Thomas's sermon, it was his reference in the Appendix to an article in the *Monmouthshire Beacon* on Saturday, 14 December, 1839 which had discussed the Chartist Rising and had quoted some statistics of church and chapel attendances from an article in the *Standard* newspaper. The statistics revealed how many more Nonconformists there were than Anglicans in Pontypool in 1839. The attendance figures told Thomas nothing that he did not already know and they only anticipated the findings of the *Religious Census* of 1851 by twelve years. In fact the position would have been worse for Anglicans in 1851 had the Chartist Rising not precipitated an improvement in the ecclesiastical re-organisation of Pontypool.

In 1839, the whole of the area north of Pontypool subsequently served by the parishes of Trevethin, Pontnewynydd and Abersychan as well as the Church of St James in Pontypool, was served by three curates of the parish of Llanover. In the same area, there were twenty-two Nonconformist chapels some of which had several hundred members, and fourteen of them were Welsh chapels "with average congregations amounting to four thousand." There was one National Anglican school at Pontypool with 180 pupils, but there were two thousand scholars in twenty-two Nonconformist Sunday schools both Welsh and English. There were two Anglican Sunday Schools with 250 scholars between them.

Thomas knew that these figures were correct and he also knew that everyone who lived in the parish of Trevethin was a parishioner and assumed to be a member of the Church of England unless that person had consciously become a Nonconformist. Under these circumstances, Thomas was riled by critics who claimed that the Nonconformists had failed to use their superior influence in chapels and Sunday schools to impart "that religious and moral instruction which is necessary to knit together the inhabitants and classes of a great country." He therefore went on to show that it was the Church of England that really failed "to bring under the influence of the

Gospel more than about one tenth of her own acknowledged children."

It was clearly unfair of the Establishment, obviously frightened by the Chartist Rising, to blame Nonconformity for its own failure to provide for the social and religious welfare of the new industrial society. At the same time there is a hidden truth in all the statistics, that even Thomas does not tell, and that is that there were more people in Pontypool under the influence of alcohol at that time than were ever under the influence of the Gospel in church or chapel.

Contemporary reporters characterised drunkenness as the chief feature of the social life of the district of Pontypool where there was an unusually high number of public houses and beer shops in 1839, and at least three prominent Chartists kept local beer shops in which Chartist lodges gathered. The members of those lodges were more influenced by demagogues in their cups than they were by ministers of religion. Even the impressive figures for chapel-attendance at the time did not account for more than half of the population.

❦

Four

The Cause of the Poor

IN the two years after 1839, Thomas continued to teach single-handedly at the College while the number of students steadily increased. As a Christian minister he was deeply concerned for the plight of the poor which he articulated as a priority of the Gospel. Pontypool sharpened his awareness of poverty but this was brought into focus by national agitation for the repeal of the Corn Laws and the activities of the Anti-Corn Law League.

The Corn Laws protected the selling price of home-grown wheat by imposing a sliding-scale of import duties on foreign wheat. The level of these duties depended upon the domestic price of wheat. The supporters of the League believed that this protective legislation artificially raised the selling price of bread to the poor while protecting the interests of the farmers. The Baptists of Monmouthshire gave their approval to the Anti-Corn Law League and local ministers attended a conference in Manchester in 1841 to consider the poverty caused by the Corn Laws.

Thomas published the sermon that he preached at that time on the text of Proverbs, Chapter 29, Verse 7: "The righteous considereth the cause of the poor; but the wicked regardeth not to know it." He expressed the purpose of his sermon as "a proper consideration of the cause of the poor, a test of righteous character." Thomas spoke of the evils of the Truck System for the payment of wages as well as the inadequate parliamentary representation, but he thought that the most pressing cause of distress at the time was the operation of the Corn Laws which "grind the faces of the poor."

Thomas knew that there were people, as always, who claimed that Christian Ministers should confine themselves to the discussion of Christian doctrine and its implications for the personal and domestic virtues and right relationships with their neighbours. He condemned those who believed that it was no part of a Minister's job to direct public attention to abuses in church and State. In a memorable phrase at the beginning of his sermon, he said that while the opponents of the interests of the poor claimed to be "politically religious," he did not know why people like himself who believed in freedom and popular rights, should not be "religiously political." "It appears also," he said, "to be just and proper that the, 'pastors and teachers' of the people should . . . direct the attention of their flock to the position of public affairs, and show the application of Christian principles to their civil duties and rights."

It must be said that Peel's repeal of the Corn Laws in 1846 brought no immediate benefit to the poor, but the cause of corn-law repeal was popular with the middle classes and the supporters of the Corn Laws were presented as a protectionist lobby of land-owning gentry in alliance with the Established Church.

In his sermon, Thomas listed political as well as economic reasons for the distress of the poor and he went on to become one of the first supporters in 1841 of the Complete Suffrage Union, a movement with middle-class leaders like the Anti-Corn Law League. In the *Nonconformist* of 20 October 1841, he argued that, "organic must precede commercial reform . . . so as to secure . . . the permanent commercial prosperity of the nation . . . There is no good expecting the removal of commercial restrictions by the present parliament." In other words, repeal of the Corn Laws would be best secured by meeting the democratic demands of the Chartists. Thus, Thomas showed that he had joined the middle class liberals who had held back from the physical violence of the Chartists but hoped to reconcile the aims of the working-class Chartists with the middle class desires of the free traders. There was mutual suspicion between the movements, but the Suffrage Union was strong in Pontypool and was supported by other Nonconformist Ministers as well as by the students of the Baptist College. When Thomas died forty years later, the town of Pontypool was still without a Member of Parliament.

Part Two

LAYING THE
FOUNDATIONS
1844-1854

Five

Growth of the College

THE original Baptist College building at Pontypool contained accommodation for Thomas and his family, and a hall that was used as refectory, chapel and library, with studies and bedrooms for the ten students who were there in 1838 when the original cost of £1,400 was cleared. The generous gift of 1,800 books on the death of Revd H. H. Williams of Cheltenham was made on condition that the College should accommodate them in a proper library which was built for a further £400. There was plenty of enthusiasm for the project and the debt was soon cleared and the library increased by gifts of further books from Mr J. Horsepool of Leicester and the Revd Micah Thomas.

Ten years after its foundation it was thought impossible for the college to accommodate more than a dozen students. By 1856, there were thirteen studies for students but only eleven bedrooms and still no proper lecture room. The jubilee celebrations in 1857 of the original College at Abergavenny provided the opportunity for an appeal for £1,500 to enlarge the College which had twenty students in residence in 1858 and thirty-three in 1863.

The College at Pontypool was efficiently organised from the outset by a committee which produced an annual report with a list of subscriptions and donations and an audited statement of accounts. As the 'Baptist Theological Institution' it was presented as a continuation of the Society that had originated in Abergavenny in 1807 and moved to Pontypool in 1836.

There was a remarkable continuity of officers and stability from the support of so many prominent Baptist families and local ministers. The Phillips family of Pontypool provided the treasurers for the institution from the end of its days in Abergavenny until Thomas Thomas's last days as President. The Revd Stephen Price of Abersychan was secretary to the College committee for the last thirty-seven years of his remarkable forty-seven year ministry at the English Baptist Church there. He died in 1878 soon after Thomas's retirement. The auditor of the committee's accounts for most of its time in Pontypool was Thomas Brooks Smith, the headmaster of the British School at George Street.

In 1841, the committee arranged the appointment of a second tutor to assist Thomas in providing the complete training for the students. They made a wise choice by appointing the Revd George Thomas, a native of Pembrokeshire who had trained at Bristol Baptist College. George Thomas remained at Pontypool as Classical Tutor for twenty-eight years and he and Thomas Thomas worked well together. At a time when more than usual attention had to be paid to the general education of ministerial students, George Thomas taught mathematics as well as Greek and Latin. Much time was spent in reading classical texts and much tribute was paid by the examiners to the students' proficiency in translating Plato. New Testament Greek was taught and the senior students had to learn Hebrew.

Thomas Thomas provided the theological education. He taught Old Testament to the junior students and New Testament, Doctrine and Philosophy to the seniors. Two selected students read papers to the annual meetings after 1848, one in Welsh and one in English, on subjects considered to be important to Baptist ministers at the time. The annual meeting was marked by a service in Welsh on the evening before the meeting and another in English on the morning of the meeting, both at Crane Street Chapel.

Thomas and George Thomas shared the same theological and educational outlook. They looked for the same qualities in their students: sound evangelical religious beliefs and experience linked with an earnest desire to acquire preaching ability. The authority of the Bible was absolute in all their work. Both men were criticised for teaching through the medium of the English language and for neglecting Welsh, though Welsh services were a feature of the College life. Most of their students had little general education at the start of their three-year course and their command of the English language was often weak.

For that reason, many Welsh applicants to Baptist colleges in England were rejected, with the result that only 45% of Baptist ministers ordained in England and Wales between 1830 and 1859 had received training before their ordination. It was thanks to colleges like Pontypool that the number of trained men entering the Baptist ministry between 1850 and 1875 increased to 67% but in 1859 it was remarked that no student ordained from the Baptist colleges at Haverfordwest or Pontypool was a graduate.

In his *Social History of the Nonconformist Ministry in England and Wales, 1800-1930* (Oxford, 1988), Kenneth Brown claimed that the teaching methods and principles in the training colleges "were not designed to encourage much independent thought and enquiry. In all subjects, especially in theology and Scripture study, all that was required was the rote learning of facts deemed to be irrefutable." As far as Pontypool College was concerned, the syllabus was certainly not static under Thomas Thomas, and there was much discussion of issues of current religious and political interest and concern. Papers were prepared and delivered by the students as well as the regular sermon classes which helped to make the students more articulate in their communication with the surrounding English-speaking society, where people were increasingly aware of the changes in scientific and theological thought.

At this time there were still only two tutors to deliver all teaching in limited financial circumstances, and the students all came from poor families. They had to be recommended for training by their local church and minister as well as two neighbouring ministers who had heard the candidate preach more than once and could vouch for his ability to read the Scriptures in English freely and have a fair command of that language. Every candidate was on probation for the first six months in the College before being admitted for the three-year course, which could be extended to four years for diligent students. Even then, the training was cash-led to the extent that any young man who satisfied the other requirements and brought with him a donation of £20 for College funds was admitted in preference to any other applicant.

Sometimes places at the College had to be limited because there were more applicants than the College could afford. Thomas had to write numerous letters to benefactors and subscribers and the students themselves had to undertake long and wearisome preaching tours to collect subscription. One such student set out from Ferndale in the Rhondda, to travel through Talybont and Builth to Machynlleth. No service had been arranged for him there and the most difficult part of his tour lay in persuading subscribers to part with their money. The student, Evan Jones, described how one Baptist Association chairman who was a businessman in Machynlleth, denounced denominational colleges stating "that he would subscribe no more to institutions that had no object in view but to keep tutors in good livings" and thought it "unreasonable to keep six men to teach fifty students."

The only letter that has survived between Thomas Thomas and the Revd William Roberts (the well-known preacher and bard, Nefydd) is a begging letter from Thomas on behalf of College funds. Written two years before Roberts became the South Wales Secretary for the Nonconformist schools in south Wales, Thomas reminded Roberts of the collection he had hinted he would make, for the Academy in the course of a month, "I write a line just to say that if you can do so within that time or soon after, it will be doing the institution essential service as the suspension of payment by the Bank has quite stopped our supplies at present." That letter, written in English from one Welsh-speaking Baptist minister to another in 1851, speaks volumes about the circumstances of life at the College at the time.

By the collection that he made the Revd William Roberts qualified himself for membership of the College Committee and he was one of the two preachers at the annual meeting of the Society in 1859.

Six

Fundamental Principles

THE Revd William Roberts, generally known by his bardic name of Nefydd, because he was a regular eisteddfod competitor, was one of the brightest lights in Monmouthshire for twenty years after 1845, the year in which he became minister of Salem Baptist Chapel, Blaina (Blaenau Gwent). A native of Denbighshire, Roberts had moved from Liverpool to Blaina where he remained until his death in 1872 at the age of sixty.

Not only did Salem prosper under Roberts in the best tradition of flourishing Baptist Chapels of that age, but its young minister set up a printing press, published books and journals, collected a library that included the diaries of Edmund Jones, the old prophet of the Tranch, a district south west of Pontypool, and most famously in 1853, became the agent (secretary) for South Wales of the British and Foreign Schools Society. Nefydd established Nonconformist schools and inspected them. He trained teachers for the schools and ran a night school in Blaina. His diaries are among the most fascinating sources for the history of Monmouthshire at the time.

His acceptance of the government grants for Nonconformist schools and the consequent establishment of state-school education brought Roberts into direct conflict with the first principle of the Principal at Pontypool Baptist College. Between the first and second Parliamentary Reform Acts of 1832 and 1867, the government gave grants for the provision of new schools to the two societies that were principally responsible for building them.

These bodies were the British and Foreign Schools Society, which was responsible for non-sectarian or Nonconformist schools after

Revd Williams Roberts (Nefydd), 1813-1872

1808, and the National Society set up in 1811, for promoting the education of the poor in the principles of the Established Church. Known respectively as the British Society and the National Society, the two societies were set up to provide schools on the pattern of two contemporary educationists, Joseph Lancaster, a Quaker, and Andrew Bell, a Scot who became a Church of England clergyman. Lancaster and Bell both used the monitorial system by which senior pupils or monitors were taught by the schoolmaster to teach their fellow-pupils.

Although many liberal members of the Church of England supported the British Schools and many National schools were liberal in their treatment of Nonconformist pupils, the two societies divided education along denominational lines. By accepting government grants, both societies admitted the principle of involvement by national government in the local provision of education, in the same way that the Poor Law Amendment Act of 1834 had imposed government direction of the previously parochial provision for poor relief.

Thomas Thomas was a voluntaryist in education because he believed that schools should be free from the sort of government control that was guaranteed by the acceptance of State funds for the management of the schools and the payment of the teachers. Conditions would be placed upon the training of teachers in State-controlled colleges and school inspectors, perhaps even members of the Established Church, would be imposed upon Nonconformist schools by the government.

Nonconformist schools should be as free as their Churches and in this voluntary principle of free, non-compulsory education, Thomas was ably supported in Pontypool by many Nonconformist colleagues including W. W. Phillips, William and Charles Conway and T. B. Smith, the headmaster of the British School at Pontypool, where Thomas was a regular visitor.

The next section of this chapter devotes more attention to Thomas's activities on behalf of voluntary education. Until 1870, when he was reluctantly forced to concede defeat, Thomas believed that the British schools of the Nonconformists should be organised and supported entirely by voluntary subscriptions from the Nonconformists themselves. This alone would avoid the extension of the State Churchism into the field of education.

By 1844, Thomas was becoming one of the leading figures of radical Dissent in Wales. Since April 1841 this Dissent had been assisted by the *Nonconformist*, a weekly newspaper, founded and edited by Edward Miall, a former Congregationalist minister who became a member of parliament in 1852. Miall set up the newspaper to denounce the State Church, and it became the official organ of the British Anti-State Church Association in 1844 after Miall organised a conference in London to launch the society. This society, after it was re-named the Society for the Liberation of Religion from State Patronage and Control, became popularly known as the Liberation Society.

Thomas was about the same age as Miall and he shared most of his religious, educational and political beliefs. Fundamental to these was the disestablishment of the State Church and Thomas became a committed member of the Liberation Society. He devoted much of his time to explaining to local audiences the aims of the campaign to free religion from "governmental or legislative interference." This meant that no financial support should be paid towards a State church by those people who had dissented from its membership. Thomas was the chairman of the meeting in Pontypool in 1848 that listened attentively to Edward Miall's promotion of the cause of disestablishment.

In 1848, disestablishment of the Church of England would have meant the end of a State church in England and Wales because it was inconceivable at that time that Wales should be considered separately from England in that matter.

The basic argument of the liberationists at that date was that the Church of England had no right to enjoy the financial and social privileges that it enjoyed as the State Church with bishops in the House of Lords, and royal patronage and rich endowments. In contrast, Nonconformists suffered civic disabilities for their dissent and yet outnumbered Anglicans in many parts of the country, not least in Wales as was proved to be the case in the Religious Census of 1851. After 1862, the movement gained ground in Wales to treat the Principality separately from England.

This was because there were social and economic issues in rural Wales associated with the payment of tithe and the class struggle between largely Welsh Nonconformist labourers and tenant farmers and English landlords who were Anglicans. Until 1870, it had not been the policy of the Church of England to appoint Welsh-speaking Welsh clergymen to bishoprics or parishes in Wales.

There was no corresponding movement of Welsh church defence in response to the Liberationist Society until the late nineteenth century. By that time, many of the Nonconformist disabilities had been removed and the Anglican Church in Wales had considerably improved its diocesan and parochial administration and its provision of pastoral care and worship. In Monmouthshire, then an archdeaconry of the Diocese of Llandaff, the arguments in favour of disestablishment were not made on the grounds of failure to provide worship in the Welsh language or even on the basis of class differences. It was almost entirely because the Nonconformist Churches were numerically stronger than the Church of England and better placed in the industrial areas to accommodate the rapid increase in population. The movement for disestablishment in Wales had to wait until the Liberal Party, which was prepared to support it, had gained enough seats in the general election of 1868 to make it feasible, and it gained a fillip from the disestablishment of the Church in Ireland in 1869. That was two decades away and literally a world away from the real disestablishment that would take until 1920.

Mention has already been made in Thomas's sermon against the Corn Laws in 1841, of his defence of Christian ministers who were "religiously political." Thomas's adherence to his principles often brought him persecution for the sake of righteousness.

He was never afraid to suffer for his principles, if that became necessary as it did in 1845. Thomas, together with his colleague, the Revd Stephen Price of Abersychan, and five lay friends, had warrants issued against them by the magistrates for the distraint of their goods by policemen. This was because they had refused to pay the Church Rate levied upon all parishioners in the Parish of Trevethin, for the building of a wall around the Churchyard and for the rebuilding of the parish Church.

Thomas, like Stephen Price, had a table, estimated to be worth two pounds and ten shillings (£2.50), taken from his home on 27 November 1845, and it was never recovered. It was reported later that the authorities were "rather afraid of the students", and no Pontypool auctioneer was willing to have anything to do with the sale of the goods distrained, and so a Newport auctioneer, named Pritchard, had to arrange the auction.

As the first incumbent of the newly-created parish of Trevethin, the Revd Thomas Davies could only be commended for wanting to rebuild and enlarge the old Church of St Cadoc, to fit it for its new parochial status and enable it to accommodate its rapidly-increasing population. As part of the penalty for having an Established Church, all the parishioners had to pay the rate that was levied by the parish vestry for Church restoration. Thomas and his friends refused to pay the rate that had been approved for rebuilding a Church from whose membership they had dissented, even though the restored parish Church had a fine baptismal pool for adult immersion under the font.

In 1845, opposition to the payment of Church Rates was not new, but had been active for more than a decade and had added fuel to the fire of disestablishment before 1844. Micah Thomas, Thomas's predecessor, had successfully postponed the levying of a Church Rate at the vestry meeting in Abergavenny in 1836. On 5 January 1837, at a meeting in Pontypool presided over by William Conway, William Phillips of Maesderwen proposed that pressure should be put upon the Whig government to act more swiftly to abolish Church Rate. After the meeting had voted to condemn Church Rate on a motion proposed by Charles Conway and seconded by Thomas Morris, Minister of the Tabernacle Chapel, Crane Street, Thomas Thomas proposed the formation of the Pontypool Church Rate Abolition Society, and his proposal was accepted.

To describe Thomas, the Principal of the Baptist College or President of the Institution, as he was described at the time, as a man of principles is to resort to platitudes. He had many clear principles which will be more clearly identified in his writings, as described later. His place in the mainstream of Protestant Dissent is assessed in the final chapter, but it can be acknowledged here that he was an evangelical Baptist Christian leader whose principles were derived from an absolute allegiance to Jesus Christ, his Lord and Saviour, the incarnate Son of God. All ecclesiastical authority for Thomas was to be found in the Holy Scriptures and most of his preaching was simple, straightforward expository preaching. Like Chaucer's poor parson, "Christ's lore, and his apostles twelve, he taught, and first he followed it himself." Thomas practised what he preached.

In some respects, Thomas was exactly what people expected of a Welsh Baptist minister of the nineteenth century. He did not smoke, he did not drink alcohol and he did not swear. He had running battles with his students about the strict prohibition of smoking on the college premises. It is alleged that he was outwitted on one occasion by students caught smoking in the boiler house who insisted that they were not smoking *on* but *under* the premises.

Like so many Victorian clergymen, Thomas was a fervent supporter of the Temperance movement. He advocated total abstinence from all alcoholic beverages and his experience of Pontypool only strengthened his opinion of the baneful effects of alcohol on the poor people of a town with so many public houses and beer shops. Yet at this distance in time, it is not always appreciated how much in advance of his own denomination Thomas was in his advocacy of total abstinence from alcoholic drinks. Although there were leading individual Baptist ministers who supported the cause of temperance throughout the nineteenth century, the Baptists were not the leaders in the field. Thomas's influence has been claimed for the greater support given to temperance in Monmouthshire by the Baptists rather than by the other denominations. In the county where Baptist ministers were foremost in the cause, Thomas was regarded as a leader. He influenced other leaders, like his own successor as Principal of the Baptist College, William Edwards, to decide in favour of abstinence. In 1907, the Baptist Union Temperance Association publicly acknowledged his contribution on the certificate that was published. As a pioneer of the pledge, Thomas played a leading role in setting up a temperance society in Pontypool as early as 1837.

On one occasion Thomas was invited to deliver a Welsh lecture on total abstinence at the Old Court Farm, Llanover, where the 'all-Welsh' rule of Lady Llanover prevailed. Whatever part Thomas might have played in preserving Lady Llanover's avowed policy of total abstinence, he did not please one Welsh listener. The man complained to the *Monmouthshire Merlin* of the bulk of statistics that Thomas had taken from English newspapers in support of his thesis, and quoted them in English with a total disregard for the Welsh language that was the medium of the lecture. For Thomas, the message was always more important than the medium. He had already been criticised for not teaching through the medium of Welsh in the Baptist College, and the Baptists were pioneers in the use of English to minister to the anglicised immigrants of industrial Monmouthshire.

The text on which Thomas expounded most in the cause of temperance was Romans, Chapter 14, Verse 21: "It is good neither to eat flesh, nor drink wine, nor anything whereby thy brother stumbleth or is offended, or is made weak." This was a text from the Authorised Version of the Bible that Thomas had been expounding for twenty years, before he appeared on platforms with Nonconformist colleagues and Anglican vicars, at the opening of Temperance Halls in the heady days of co-operation over such social matters in the late 1850s.

In July 1858, Thomas stood shoulder to shoulder with John Griffith, then Vicar of Aberdare, as well as the Wesleyan Methodist minister and his Baptist colleague and former student, Thomas Price, for the opening of the Temperance Hall at Aberdare. He did likewise at Tredegar in 1861, where his eloquent and "pithy remarks were received with rounds of applause", and Thomas was listened to attentively because "he had been an abstainer during his whole lifetime, being then an aged and revered person."

The "aged and revered person" was then fifty-six and the continuation of his story shows Thomas's life-long opposition to the "drink that inebriates" as it was called. The real development in his thinking came when Thomas was in his early forties. He had supported the poor in his opposition to the Corn Laws as well as in his support of universal male suffrage. He had exonerated Nonconformists from the charge of sedition by denying their alleged involvement in the Newport Rising of 1839. At the same time, Thomas had reminded dissenters of their civic responsibilities and the authority and power of the civil government to punish offenders. He had asserted the freedom of Nonconformists to organise their own religious education in church and school without government interference and to refuse financial support for the State Church from which they had dissented.

At that point, Thomas applied the logic of his passive resistance by insisting that the magistrate exceeded his brief when he interfered with the freedom of a person's religious conscience. By asserting his right to refuse to pay the Church Rate through conscientious objection, Thomas passively accepted the right of the magistrate to distrain on his property for recovery of the payment. The matter was not as clear-cut as Thomas would have liked it to be.

The issue in Thomas's mind was not the need to set and levy a rate from every person in the parish for the maintenance of a Church of which every citizen had lawful use, not least for the burial of family members, but the denial of a right for Nonconformists to be buried by their own ministers according to their own rites. This was a right granted in 1880, that Thomas only just lived to see. Was his refusal to pay a temporal tax really justified because it was used to finance what was for him a continuing spiritual disability?

Certainly Thomas thought so in 1846 and 1847 when he and his friends in Pontypool were fighting for the principle of voluntaryism in education, the right of Nonconformists to organise and finance their own schools by voluntary contributions free from State control. Thomas was a member of the committee that had formally opened the British School in Pontypool on 20 July 1843 when seventy children were admitted. He had helped to interview Mr T. B. Smith for the post of headmaster, a position Smith held for over forty years as well as being superintendent of the Sunday school at Crane Street Chapel.

Thomas was a regular visitor to the school and it greatly saddened him to have to sever his connections with its management committee when his colleagues voted to accept the government grant for the school that they could not afford to refuse after 1870. In 1847, at an important meeting about education at Pontypool, Thomas secured the passing of five resolutions that upheld the voluntary principle in education. The result of this was that in the district from Abergavenny to Llantarnam, there were very few British schools because government grants were refused. Nefydd lamented this fact several times in his diary.

On 30 January 1862, he wrote that the British School at Llantarnam with 120 pupils was the envy of church people. It stood on the edge of a large district of twenty thousand people where there were twelve National Schools with 1,200 pupils "and that chiefly through the influence of our great voluntary educationist, T. Thomas D.D., Pontypool College." Nefydd noted that there were at least four dissenters for every one churchman in the district, but the workmen who would gladly have welcomed a British School, as at Pontrhydyrun, could not do so against the wishes of managers and proprietors who were influenced by Dr Thomas.

In his resolutions of 1847 Thomas stated "That it forms no part of the ordinary duty of civil government to train the mind of the people", because government interference in such important work was a threat both to parental rights and to civil and religious liberty. The best thing that the government could do for education, said Thomas, was to remove the taxes. He believed that the religion of

Nonconformist schools would be compromised by receiving government grants because they would be open to government inspectors who represented an alien church establishment. Nonconformists should finance their own schools in the same way that they provided chapels or theological colleges. State churchism should not be let in through government grants.

Thomas's resolutions were disliked by Jelinger Symons, a young barrister serving as one of the government commissioners enquiring into the state of education in Monmouthshire. The Committee of Council that appointed Symons looked forward to a separate report on Monmouthshire partly because of the reactions in the county to the Minutes of Council for 1846 which provoked Thomas to issue his resolutions.

Although Monmouthshire was not at that time normally included with Welsh affairs, it was recognised that the parishes in the county that were part of the South Wales Coalfield should be included in the enquiry to give a complete picture of the state of education in the mining community. When the Reports of the Commissioners were published, they were almost a self-fulfilling prophecy of what had been said by the Home Secretary in the House of Commons. This was in response to William Williams, the Welsh-born member of parliament for Coventry, who requested the enquiry, "that their (the Welsh people's) ignorance greatly interferes with their prosperity, and prevents them rising in the scale of society: and I regret to say that in some parts of the Principality, the ignorance of the people not only lowers them intellectually, but depraves their moral qualities."

These last four words, as they worked out in the details of the Report, were what caused most offence, especially when it was stated that poor living conditions were proof of moral degeneracy in a society where Welsh Nonconformity had a predominant influence. It was small wonder that the Revd John Griffith as the new Vicar of Aberdare aroused the ire of the Revd Thomas Price, Baptist bishop of Aberdare and Thomas Thomas's star pupil, because of the evidence against his parishioners that Griffith gave to the Commissioners.

The Report of the Education Commissioners castigated Non-conformity and the Welsh language as well as the morality of the Welsh people. The report, which became known as *Brad y Llyfrau Gleision* (Treason of the Blue Books) was published in three volumes in the late autumn of 1847. It provoked much response. Thomas spoke against its contents at a meeting in Cardiff, but his time that autumn was taken with preparing for a series of eight lectures that were advertised in the *Nonconformist* on 13 October 1847 and delivered in Pontypool and Newport in November and December. The lectures were given by Thomas and a number of other Non-conformist ministers, including Evan Jones (Ieuan Gwynedd) of Tredegar and Thomas L. Bright of Newport, both Independent ministers, and David D. Evans, Baptist minister of Pontrhydyrun. Advertised as "a course of lectures on the present duties devolving on Christian professors", their purpose was to explain to local audiences in Pontypool and Newport the campaign of the Anti-State Church Association. The lecturers were all members of that association as well as being voluntaryists in education.

Seven

The Voluntaryist in Pontypool

I N the first lecture of the series Thomas objected to government interference in the education of children and in the training of their teachers. In a long discourse on "the duty of religious men to study the times in which they live, and to apply their energies to the right conduct of public affairs", Thomas condemned the "new education scheme . . . which . . . infringes upon civil liberty, tends to subvert parental responsibility and rears a new church establishment for the religious education of the rising generation." This was the same establishment that he denigrated seven years later as "the educational Church establishment in the Borough Road", a reference to the training college for teachers established in Borough Road, Isleworth, London, by the British and Foreign Schools Society.

The themes of Thomas's first lecture were the voluntary principle and Thomas's reasons for preferring voluntaryism in church and school. The value of the voluntary principle had been demonstrated by the rapid spread of Christianity in the first three hundred years of the Christian era, said Thomas, "and the decline of paganism by the energies of the voluntary principle, not only without the aid, but in spite of the hostility of all the governments of the world." Thomas took the view that voluntaryism was only undermined by "the unholy alliance of nominal Christianity with the secular government first introduced by Constantine the Great", and leading later to the establishment of the papacy in the middle ages.

The reformation heralded "glorious signs of progress", through "men of whom the world was not worthy; who combining piety and patriotism, changed the face of Europe, and opened up for degraded humanity a blissful prospect . . .". These were the men who "called on nations to shake off their fetters, and have guided their struggles against ecclesiastical and civil despotism."

Thomas knew that there would always be people who thought that ministers of religion should have nothing to do with politics, but he insisted that a man was not divested of the rights and responsibilities of a citizen when he became a minister of the Gospel, and since our conduct in this life would determine our state in the next, it must surely be the duty of the Christian ministry to point out to people the duties and dangers of membership of a civil community. Without neglecting their religious duties, thought Thomas, ministers should sometimes help to improve their neighbours' welfare and discuss questions of social responsibility as they affected citizens and churches.

The Hebrew prophets had shown that there was no natural opposition between secular and religious affairs, but that religious influence could be usefully exerted on the government. The Bible provided many examples of religious men exerting influence on national affairs, from Joseph to Nicodemus and Joseph of Arimathea. Christian history provided examples in Luther, Melanchthon, Calvin and Zwingli, though they made a serious mistake in Thomas's eyes by "seeking the re-establishment of state-Churchism in the shape of Protestantism and Reform."

The princes who favoured the cause of these reformers should, thought Thomas, have been instructed to "free Christianity from state patronage and control." In seventeenth century England, the great men of the Commonwealth were "Christian politicians instead of sectarian monopolists", and they did not believe that they had compromised their religious character by the part that they took in national affairs. In the same way, claimed Thomas, modern dissenters had played a great part in "parliamentary reform, the repeal of the Catholic disabilities, the abolition of slavery, and monopoly, and the diffusion of knowledge and Christianity."

The severest critics of the politics of Dissent said Thomas had been the "zealous partisans of a political church, whose very bishops are legislators; whose services, articles, canons, courts and revenues are all regulated by law; whose special acts of public devotion in fasts and thanksgivings are directed by royal authority; whose priests are found on boards of guardians, and on the bench of magistrates; and to whom it appertains to consecrate military banners in order to sanctify the trade of war, and to render public thanks to Almighty God for the happy issue of battles which have covered countries with carnage and coloured rivers with human blood!"

Thomas went on to outline the characteristics of the contemporary scene as he understood them and the duty of religious men towards them. The outstanding characteristic was the conflict between civil liberty and arbitrary power.

Thomas highlighted the triumph of liberty through the:

> general freedom of the press in Britain;
> extension of the franchise in the large towns;
> reforms of the corporations;
> civil registration of births, marriages and deaths;
> improvement of the criminal code and penal laws;
> increasingly strong public aversion towards capital punishment and to the game laws;
> abolition of the slave trade and of slavery itself in the British colonies and the progress then being made on that issue in Europe and the United States of America;
> penny postage;
> repeal of the Corn Laws accompanied by the rapid spread of the doctrine of free trade.

All those matters constituted a check-list of what had been achieved in the name of progress through the alliance of evangelical Dissenters with the political priorities of Whig governments between 1830 and 1845. There was much unfinished business, notably in the abolition of Church Rate, which would have to wait until 1868, and the burial of Nonconformists by their own rites in parish churchyards, which was not possible before 1880.

In anticipation of what would happen in Europe in 1848, Thomas proclaimed that France, Germany, Switzerland and Italy were in ferment while chaos reigned in Spain and Portugal. In those countries in 1847, Thomas was not "celebrating the triumphs of civil liberty" but "contemplating its struggles—its successful but very arduous struggles—with arbitrary power." In Britain, there were examples, he said, of the tendency of government to curtail popular rights in the administration of the Poor Law and the "recent scheme of educational patronage" by the committee of Council. He went on to say that, "the extension of government influence over religious sects by means of state endowments is equally hostile" to civil and religious liberty because, "religious equality is essential to civil liberty."

Thomas was a pacifist and he regretted the increasing military strength of Britain, "with a huge standing army in times of domestic peace . . . kept in comparative idleness and vice, supported at an enormous expense by a nation overburdened with debts and taxes, distributed like garrisons in multiplying barracks all over the country . . .". Thomas thought that such a military presence was hardly calculated to give people a high opinion of their civil liberty.

Thomas rejoiced that the unscriptural and harmful effects of the union of State and Church were justly perceived in 1847. He praised the examples of the United States of America and the impression made upon the Christian world by America's separation of religion from the state, and the development of the principle of voluntaryism in that vast country under unfavourable circumstances. This proved that civil government and religion could prosper together without a legal alliance between them.

Thomas praised the work of the Anti-State Church Association as well as the general opposition to Church Rates by ratepayers in the towns, and the way in which Dissenters secured the return to parliament of MPs dedicated to the causes of dissent, voluntaryism and religious liberty. At the same time he realised the power of the opposition they faced from the supporters of the State Church.

State Churchism was "venerable for its antiquity having existed under some Christian form ever since the time of Constantine the Great . . . it still possesses great power and its adherents will not give it up without a desperate struggle." Their resources, concluded Thomas, were immense.

Thomas condemned the insidious State Churchism exemplified by the creation of more bishoprics in England and the ecclesiastical centralisation and patronage system in Britain. He criticised the grants to the, "three denominations", from the *Regium Donum* since the time of Queen Anne, and the distribution of parliamentary grants. Thomas concluded that Christian patriots should have nothing to do with such grants but should unite in peaceful measures for the liberation of religion from state control and to give full scope to the free working of the voluntary principle everywhere. Thomas noted that educational provision had improved and that there was an increase of knowledge, particularly among the poor. The Dissenters had done most for that section of society, but they were denounced for objecting to "government interference with instruction, and to the payment of teachers as tending to create a spirit of dependence and subserviency." Only by refusing all government grants could liberty be preserved.

In Thomas's view, the government should not interfere with education. They should neither pay the teachers nor impose taxes upon the means of instruction. Such a vision of an educational system free from becoming the political football of successive governments has its own dream-like fascination at the start of the second millennium, but such an aspiration was sadly utopian though never divorced from the reality of educational debate for Thomas in 1847. Voluntary societies, he believed, should be encouraged at local and national level so that competent teachers could be trained to provide cheap or free education for the children of the poor.

Thomas's personal version of the Victorian gospel of progress found evidence for the victory of the Christian faith and the increasing confidence commanded in the Bible by "the great, the wise and the good" in society. He believed that infidelity, as preached by the instigators of the French Revolution and by such radical freethinkers as Richard Carlile, Reverend Robert Taylor or Robert Owen, was in decline. Robert Taylor was a lapsed clergyman who joined Richard Carlile in the 1820s in trying to undermine the Bible and its defenders. Thomas believed that the Bible had overcome infidelity and sound evangelical views had triumphed over the "neological doctrines of Germany."

Yet although evangelical faith had overcome infidelity, Thomas was shrewd enough to realise that the opposite evil, superstition, still remained. Unintelligent faith had often degenerated into superstition, into which category, in an unecumenical age, Thomas placed the Roman Catholic Church and the activities of the Jesuits as well as the darkness of "heathen lands afar" such as India. Yet Thomas thought that faith was gaining ground over superstition.

Thomas ended on an optimistic note by highlighting the co-operation and unity he had observed among evangelical Christians "in Bible, missionary, tract, temperance and education societies." He thought that this co-operation could be carried much further among all Christians "but for the existence of that great stumbling-block, a State Church, and the vexatious application of the compulsory principle which compels all to support one favoured sect." Thus at the conclusion of his peroration, Thomas demonstrated that this lecture was not intended to frighten Jelinger Symons, though it might have done so, but to gladden the heart of Edward Miall.

Eight

What is a Nonconformist?

O N 21 December 1847 at Pontypool, Thomas delivered the seventh lecture in the series. He described the lecture as observations on the "Christian duty on determined adherence to right principles", and he introduced it with a text from the Book of Job in the Old Testament: "Till I die I will not remove mine integrity from me: my righteousness I hold fast and will not let it go" (Job 27: 5-6). So the scene was set for a full-scale defence of integrity and no single piece of contemporary writing provides a better illustration of what it meant to be a Nonconformist in Wales in the mid-nineteenth century, the finest hour that Nonconformity has ever known.

Dramatic irony decrees that December 21 in the Book of Common Prayer was a red-letter feast day of St Thomas the Apostle. Thomas Thomas was no 'doubting Thomas' in his refusal to conform to the Prayer Book of the Established Church. In writing of Thomas at this time, one of Wales's best historians, Ieuan Gwynedd Jones, has described him as "an archetypal Welsh Nonconformist." That is true only in the sense that Thomas Thomas, was a perfect example of what it meant to be a Nonconformist. If the adjective presupposes no antecedents, then it is incorrect. Thomas was rooted in the Puritan tradition. His indebtedness to that tradition emerges clearly from this lecture which is a justification—scriptural, historical and spiritual—of the Nonconformist position.

The principles of Nonconformists, or Voluntaries, as Thomas called them, should be communicated, he said, without fear of *agitation* because "no great good has ever been, or can be, done without it." From the beginning, said Thomas, the Gospel provoked opposition and was a cause of conflict. Jesus warned that this would be so and examples of opposition are provided in the New Testament. By acting according to the same principles as the first Christians, we suffer as they did.

Thomas believed that it was essential to communicate Nonconformist principles to the rising generation. In a world where people who were willing to be awkward for their principles would not be popular, it could be expected that young people would take the way of easy conformity to the State Church for the sake of social acceptance and career prospects. Nonconformist parents should teach their children why they had dissented from the Church of England. This had clearly not been happening, so that the children were not prepared to be despised by socially superior Anglicans, nor ready to sacrifice success in their trade or profession for their principles.

Evangelical dissent presented a great challenge to the children of Nonconformists because it challenged their worldly wisdom and ambitions and was not easily inherited in families, but depended upon conversions. For that reason, said Thomas, the "morally corrupt, and the sentimentally and superficially pious among our descendants naturally renounce the religion of their parents, and adopt one more congenial to their passions and interests."

He therefore thought that the heads of Nonconformist families should train their children in the principles of dissent. Similarly in day schools and Sabbath schools and certainly in dissenting colleges, young people should be taught dissenting principles, "that Christianity may be seen . . . in her heavenly simplicity and beauty . . .".

Thomas did not underestimate the power of the Press as a medium that was generally opposed to Nonconformists, but could be used in defence of dissent. A number of newspapers and magazines were in sympathy with Nonconformity and could be used to defend and promote the principles of dissent. These principles would be upheld with integrity through the authority of the dissenter's conscience under the authority of God. For that reason the civil magistrate could have no authority in religious matters and

Nonconformists should not observe the "sacred times and seasons prescribed by law," because that involved a distinct recognition of the magistrate's authority in religious affairs.

The magistrate could not command the Christian to observe Christmas Day, Easter or other ordinary festivals or fasts and thanksgiving days. Christians should decide according to their consciences whether or not to obey demands of the civil government in matters of religion. They should not refuse to obey the secular authority for the sake of disobedience, but they should act according to their consciences because Nonconformists recognised the principle of obedience to the magistrate in matters of conscience while reserving to themselves the right to decide whether the order was good or bad.

Above all, said Thomas, as he moved to the most important outcome of the application of Nonconformist principles, "A consistent adherence to right principles involves the withholding of all active support of a State Church as the practical embodiment of all those principles which are opposed to them."

Thomas believed that the other lecturers in the series, Evan Jones (Ieuan Gwynedd) Independent minister of Tredegar, Thomas L. Bright, Independent minister of Commercial Street, Newport and his Baptist colleagues, Stephen Price of Abersychan, David Evans of Pontrhydyrun and George Thomas of the Baptist College, had proved that it was immoral to enforce upon people allegiance to religion. Thomas believed that such compulsion was offensive to God and man because it denied freedom of conscience and supported tyranny, oppression, contention, formality, subserviency, hypocrisy and persecution.

For those who dissented from the State Church there awaited insults, distraints, loss of employment, confiscation of property, imprisonment and even death. But since dissenters believed that a State Church was morally wrong, how could they support financially what was morally wrong? The State's demand for the payment of a Church Rate was morally wrong and the dissenter was morally obliged to refuse payment, although he was, in Thomas's view, morally obliged to pay legitimate taxes for secular purposes.

It was, Thomas declared, a sin to defraud the Revenue by making a false income tax return or to encourage black market trading. But a specific tax for religious purposes was a different matter because it affected God and the individual conscience. Christians could not render to Caesar what belonged to God, he said. In this respect Thomas had not moved since his Chartist sermon in 1839. If a man believed that it was contrary to his Christian conscience to pay taxes for ecclesiastical purposes, then he should refuse payment and submit to the consequences or he would violate his principles by doing what was morally wrong. This was the doctrine of passive resistance or what Thomas called "passive obedience."

In support of his view, Thomas quotes Robert Hall, foremost Baptist preacher of his day, who had died in 1831 and whose sermons had been published in 1843. He also quotes John Bunyan as saying "when I cannot obey actively, then I am willing to lie down and to suffer what they shall do to me." Among non-Baptists, Thomas finds support in the refusal of the Presbyterian Professor John Brown of Edinburgh, to pay the annual tax in support of the Presbyterian State Clergy, which he justified in a valuable work that he published on "the Law of Christ respecting Civil Obedience." The example of the Society of Friends is also cited in defence of Thomas's principle of passive obedience and willingness to face the consequences without resistance. Quaker authors quoted by Thomas included Thomas Clarkson who had worked for the abolition of the slave trade and died in 1846, and Joseph John Gurney of Norwich, who died in 1847, another abolitionist and prison reformer like his wife, Elizabeth Fry.

Thomas estimated that Quakers had lost between ten and twelve thousand pounds a year from distraints on their property through refusal to comply with ecclesiastical demands. Their losses for conscience sake had been incalculable, and they were being followed by an increasing number of other dissenters including numerous Church Rate victims, many of whom had been put in gaol.

Thomas regarded such resistance as effective because "By such non-compliance with the demand for a Church Rate in this Parish (Trevethin), a blow has been given to the anti-Christian system which has resounded through the land. Convinced of the rectitude of that step, we review it with satisfaction, and say to our country-men, Go you, and do likewise."

This same principle of freedom of conscience should apply also to the exercise of the vote in an election, said Thomas. If the freedom of the individual before God in the matter of religion is the most important principle of all for dissenters or voluntaryists, then no dissenter could use his vote to assist State Churchism. In Parliament, no dissenter could possibly use his vote to support the continuation of an Established Church. As a parliamentary elector no dissenter could vote for a candidate who supported the Established Church.

Nonconformists, said Thomas, could not go on professing to believe in principles which they did not effectively support if they, "practically uphold an ecclesiastical monopoly which cherishes the most inveterate worldliness with its concomitant evils under the mask of religious profession." Thomas reserved his most bitter criticism for his fellow dissenters who boasted of their Nonconformist "ancestors and martyrs, and then prove how unworthy we are of them by pursuing a course the very reverse of that in which they suffered, bled, and died."

Thus Nonconformists' adherence to right principles should be shown by actively propagating them and by withholding all aid from the contrary principles. The State Church should not be supported either by money or by the vote. Thomas castigated the "Vicar of Bray" capacity of the clergy of the Church of England to remain in their livings throughout the vicissitudes and changes of the English Reformation whether Henry VIII or Mary was on the throne.

But he did that only to remind his contemporary Nonconformist ministers that their own conduct often demonstrated equal inconsistencies and anomalies. If they accepted the principle that there should be no state interference in religion but bowed to the authority of the magistrate by paying Church Rates, by observing "the customary or special fasts and festivals with even greater solemnity than the Lord's Day," and by going to the Established Church when they attained certain honours or offices or for marriages and burials, their behaviour was inconsistent. If dissenters complained about clergymen of the Church of England because they refused bells or burial in the Churchyard to unbaptised people, they should not go seeking the services of those same clergymen for themselves. Dissenters should maintain those noble principles of Christian freedom which they had learned from the Bible and retain their integrity with dignity, said Thomas.

Thomas went on to his final observation that Nonconformists must stand firm against the blackmail and bribery that were used to gain votes at elections for the parliamentary candidates of the landlords. Those who stood firm by their principles might be in a minority but "truth, justice and victory do not always go with the majority." In spite of what Carlyle had said about the demise of the age of the Puritans, said Thomas, Puritanism "has never yet been dead, but only dormant." "Yes," he concluded, "there are men amongst us still who are Puritans in everything except the name." Principles were more important than numbers. A man's convictions would inspire him with confidence especially when he believed that "the cause he has espoused is the cause of God."

This, said Thomas, was the secret of the martyrs, exemplified in Luther's behaviour at the Diet of Worms and described by Milton in the character of Abdiel at the end of Book V of *Paradise Lost*:

> Abdiel faithful found
> Among the faithless, faithful only he;
> Among innumerable false, unmov'd,
> Unshaken, unseduced, unterrified,

His loyalty he kept, his love, his zeal;
Nor number, nor example with him wrought
To swerve from truth, or change his constant mind.

Such was the character of the Nonconformist, but in exhorting others to embrace it, Thomas was acknowledging its antecedents and aligning himself with those who shared it. He was thus not the originator of the Nonconformity he represented though he was certainly a model of such Puritanism and in many respects its last example. Nor was he alone in the presentation of those lectures that were deemed so potentially threatening to the educational establishment at the time. He was well supported by able Nonconformist colleagues among Independents and Baptists, the two most radical denominations at the time.

As can be observed, the lectures are much less to do with the immediate problems presented by the enquiries of the educational commissioners and much more to do with the defence of voluntaryism and the iniquities of an Established Church. The final thought of Thomas's last lecture in this series is the one that would most commend itself to fair-minded Christians in any century.

He claimed that it would be a public benefit to liberate Christianity from the interference of the government because the principal reason for not conforming would have been removed in a disestablished Church. Thomas envisaged a disestablished Church in which her bishops and clergy were relieved of their secular responsibilities and subserviency to lay patrons. Under such circumstances, the disestablished Church would become simpler in its behaviour and worship. She could co-operate on equal terms with other Churches and they could sit down together to plan the real work of evangelism.

It has since become clear that this most commendable of truths would sadly be the most regrettable victim of the hostility aroused by the disestablishment campaign. It would take much longer to achieve than Christians had hoped.

Part Three

THE MIDDLE YEARS
1854-1870

Nine

Family Life

A MAN born in 1805 would have been flattered to be thought middle-aged in his forties when most of his contemporaries were going to the grave at that age. For Thomas Thomas, the years between 1854 and 1870 represented a period of middle age and growing old. His middle years coincided with the middle period of Victoria's reign, designated by W. L. Burn as the Age of Equipoise. How gracefully Thomas grew old is open to question and with how much equilibrium this chapter may reveal.

Throughout these years, Thomas and his wife Mary continued to live in the accommodation provided at the Baptist College on Penygarn. Their three sons, Llewellyn, William and Thomas Henry lived with them as well as their two nieces, Anne and Emily Henry, the daughters of Mrs Thomas's younger sister Jane. In addition to the family, a cook, a housemaid and often one other servant lived in the President's accommodation as well as six college students. After a successful general appeal for money that owed much to the personal efforts of Thomas himself, student accommodation at the college improved after 1856 and by 1858, student numbers had reached the record number to date of twenty.

The number of Baptist ministers who received college training in the 1850s increased from 45% to 67% and that was almost exactly the same as the percentage of new Baptist ministers who originated in Wales in the thirty years after 1840. Many of those Welsh ministers had been refused training in Hoxton or Bristol because of their poor command of English. That helps to explain the emphasis upon English at Pontypool College for which Thomas was criticised in *Seren Gomer* in 1854.

Mary Thomas, 1805-1881
(Courtesy, South Wales Baptist College, Cardiff)

Thomas's predecessor, Micah Thomas had been similarly criticised at Abergavenny and perhaps the sudden death of Micah Thomas at the end of 1853 triggered the reminder of such battles in the past. Thomas Thomas preached at the funeral of his old mentor at Abergavenny on 5 December 1853 and later helped to divide his large library between the Baptist colleges of Haverfordwest and Pontypool.

At Pontypool, Thomas's sons, Llewellyn and William were as old as the college students and William had just begun training for the ministry. Llewellyn, who had laid the foundation stone of the college at the tender age of five, had become a local chemist. On 8 January 1854, Llewellyn died at the college at the age of twenty-two from consumption. Within four months, William had died of the same disease at the age of nineteen. The *Monmouthshire Merlin* on 5 May described William as a young man of "no ordinary abilities, of genuine piety and of great promise . . . much endeared to his family and respected and beloved by all who knew him." Like so many other families in Pontypool and elsewhere at that time, Thomas and Mary Thomas had to watch while the dreaded tuberculosis carried off their children and during the next two years, their two nieces Anne and Emily Henry, also.

At a national level an unexplained decline in tuberculosis began during the 1850s but, as they would say in Pontypool 'there was a lot of it about.' Even allowing for the household of faith in which these deaths occurred and Victorian expectations of such sadness because killer diseases held sway these tragic deaths hit hard. The loss of two sons in the springtime of their lives followed by the deaths of two dependent nieces came as a great shock to Thomas and Mary Thomas.

Their youngest son, Thomas Henry, born at the college in the year of the Chartist rising in Newport, was away at school in Bristol when his brothers died. Better known later by his bardic name, Arlunydd Penygarn, Thomas Henry Thomas was a famous artist who became associated with Welsh cultural life as a painter and a naturalist. His education took him to Paris and Rome. After his father's death in Cardiff, Thomas Henry, who had finally settled there himself, wrote a very good short account of his father's life that was published in the volume of *Welsh Religious Leaders in the Victorian Era* edited by J. Vyrnwy Morgan in 1905. Given the times and the closeness of the writer to his subject, the objectivity of the account says much for the intelligence of the artist.

About his own feelings at the deaths of his brothers, Thomas Henry Thomas is silent, but of its effects on his parents' lives he is clear:

"In 1854-55, Thomas Thomas passed through a period of bitter sorrow: two sons, Llewellyn and William Thomas, died within a few months of one another. Both were excellent young men, the second possessed great intellectual gifts, and was a student for the ministry. Their loss cast a cloud over their parents' lives, followed as it was by the death of two nieces living with them."

Small wonder that in the wake of this tragedy, Thomas Thomas contemplated leaving Pontypool for a pastorate in London. The students at the college played their part in keeping him in Pontypool as he launched himself into the campaign to improve and extend the college accommodation. This work was completed by 1857 in time for the celebrations to mark the golden jubilee of the original foundation at Abergavenny.

Ten

The Family at Crane Street

HE personal sorrows of Thomas Thomas and his family
were set against a national backcloth of war in the Crimea,
which subsequently provided a suburb of Pontypool with
the unlikely name of Sebastopol. The mood of Pontypool during
the war years was one of rejoicing after the birth of John Capel
Hanbury, son and heir to the seventy-six-year-old squire of the
Hanbury estate, Capel Hanbury Leigh. The celebrations included
the roasting in Pontypool Park of a whole ox which was then
distributed to an estimated crowd of twenty thousand people!

The proud father paid for the building of the original town hall
in Pontypool in thanksgiving for his son's birth and his mother laid
the foundation stone on his first birthday in 1854. The *Monmouthshire Merlin* reported that the new town hall satisfied the long-felt
popular need for a building where important questions might be
discussed and business transacted while knowledge was acquired
and taste gratified. With barely a foundation stone laid, the *Merlin*
created a castle in the air where a Mayor of Pontypool, surrounded
by Alderman and Councillors could sit in civic state. Christian
patriots and eloquent philanthropists would deliver diatribes where
science would "have her numerous votaries," and "sweet song
entrance the listening multitude and moral conversation gladden
the hearts of the toilers," in the imagination of the *Monmouthshire
Merlin*.

Had the reporter of the *Monmouthshire Merlin* walked a few
hundred yards into nearby Crane Street, he would have seen a fine
classical building designed by J. H. Langdon and built in 1847 at the
large cost of £2,200, which exceeded the initial outlay for the town

Crane Street Baptist Chapel, Pontypool

hall. Crane Street Baptist Chapel had a narrower but nevertheless what Anthony Jones has called "a dramatic and dominating street presence." It was built from the subscriptions of £1,000, collected by the congregation that had been meeting since 1836 in the Meeting House of the Society of Friends (Quakers) in Trosnant. The original Church consisted of only sixteen members, including Thomas and Mary Thomas, who had covenanted together to form an English Baptist Church for the benefit of Baptists who had moved to Pontypool and spoke no Welsh.

Upper Trosnant Baptist Chapel, Pontypool

When the Religious Census was taken in 1851, Crane Street was among the smaller Chapels of South Wales. There were at least three larger Baptist Chapels in Pontypool, Trosnant (later called Upper Trosnant), Zion Chapel Trosnant, which merged with Crane Street in 1878, and Tabernacle, also in Crane Street with services in Welsh, which was demolished to make a car park in 1970. Crane Street still survives in all its classical splendour, hemmed in by later and much inferior buildings. Its powerful pillars are replicated on the façade of the pulpit, which was designed in the form of a large platform for teaching and debate rather than oratorical preaching.

That was exactly what Thomas Thomas wanted, and his purpose of communicating light was assisted by a large and expensive glass-panelled roof. This provided daylight throughout the building through the glass floor between the Chapel and the basement hall below. The Baptistry for the baptism of members by total immersion is below the floor of the pulpit platform. The interior of the Chapel in Thomas Thomas's time was attractive but simple and included no stained glass windows or large organ or even a cross. Even so, the congregation took more than twenty years to pay off the debt incurred in 1847.

About three hundred people attended the tea and meeting at Crane Street Chapel on 7 November 1867, to celebrate the payment of the debt. Only two of the original sixteen members of 2 August 1836 then remained, namely Thomas and Mary Thomas. They had come from the Church at Henrietta Street in London. Mrs Thomas's younger sister Jane David had come from the Tabernacle Church in Cardiff. Nine members had transferred from the English Baptist Church at Abersychan including the founder of that Church, William Williams Phillips. He was the grandson of the great Miles Harry and agent to the Park Estate, and he had decided to set up an English Baptist Church in Pontypool.

Interior of Crane Street Baptist Chapel showing parts of the glass panelled roof and the gallery

William Williams Phillips died on 26 July 1860, more than a year before his illustrious employer, Capel Hanbury Leigh died from accidental poisoning in Penarth at the age of eighty-five. Phillips was ten years younger but he had served as agent of the estate even before Hanbury Leigh's appointment as Lord Lieutenant in 1835.

When Thomas Thomas gave thanks for the payment of the Chapel debt in 1867, he recalled also the debt that he and Crane Street Chapel owed to William W. Phillips, its first and only deacon for the first three years and "for twenty-four years its most influential deacon." Phillips was praised by the *Pontypool Free Press* at the time of his death as a, "warm advocate and zealous promoter of Sunday Schools without regard for denomination." Like Thomas Thomas, Phillips was a voluntaryist in education and opposed to government grants for the British School in Pontypool. He was also opposed to the levying of Church Rate although the Park estate gave £500 to the rebuilding of Trevethin Parish Church in 1846 and a parish rate was levied for the purpose.

On the occasion of the funeral of William Phillips in July 1860, Thomas Thomas travelled in the Lord Lieutenant's carriage with Sir Thomas Phillips and the incumbents of Trevethin and Panteg. Thomas conducted the service at the grave at Penygarn Chapel and preached what the *Free Press* called a "highly edifying and impressive discourse" at the memorial service in Crane Street Chapel a month later.

William W. Phillips had been a force in local affairs and in Baptist politics for more than thirty years. He went to Abersychan as Manager of the British Iron Works in 1826 and he founded the English Baptist Chapel there a year later. Before becoming agent to Capel Hanbury Leigh, he was the Manager of the Pontypool branch of the Monmouth and Glamorgan Bank and he was treasurer to the Baptist College at Abergavenny and Pontypool for thirty-one years. He obtained the rental of the Friends' Meeting House in Trosnant for the first meetings of what became Crane Street Baptist Chapel and for the rest of his life he was a deacon of the Church.

What was most impressive about Thomas's discourse at Phillips' memorial service was not the eulogy in praise of a Baptist leader whom he much admired and personally liked. It was the reminder at the end of the sermon, so characteristic of Thomas, that this was a human being whom they were remembering and Thomas was not afraid to say that.

> "There were infirmities of temper and errors of judgment. There might sometimes seem too strong a love of human approbation, and too strong a dread of human censure. There were also apparent shortcomings with regard to the development and application of the great principles of evangelical dissent, and the support of the aggressive movements for the emancipation of religion from state patronage and control, and the full establishment of Christian liberty and equality . . ." Thomas concluded that, "His faults were few and small in comparison of his excellences."

William Williams Phillips, Senior, as he was known because he had a son of the same name who also became a public figure in Pontypool, was a remarkable man. He was remarkable not least because he preserved his integrity as a faithful Nonconformist while working for the Lord Lieutenant. He served the State at a time when the radical Nonconformity of Thomas Thomas was seeking complete freedom of the Christian churches from all State patronage and control. The most testing time for William Phillips must have been the occasion to which Thomas Thomas also referred in his address at the celebration of the settlement of the Chapel debt in 1867.

That had been the occasion, already mentioned, of the public demonstration in Pontypool Park with the roasting of the ox to celebrate the birth of the son and heir to Capel Hanbury Leigh. As part of the celebrations, sports and amusements were arranged to which the Sunday School of Crane Street Chapel was invited together with the other Sunday Schools of Pontypool. On 30 May 1853, Thomas Thomas had secured a resolution in the Church meeting at Crane Street condemning the:

> "degrading and demoralising sports and amusements . . .
> because they are utterly unworthy of the intelligence and
> refinements of the present day, and tend to degrade the com-
> mon people, and to counteract the efforts made for their
> intellectual and moral improvement."

So the pastor and officers and teachers of the Sunday School did not
join the procession.

Thomas had clearly felt that the strong resolution passed by the
Church in May 1853 had asserted a puritan principle that he held
dear and he revisited the event in his address to the public meeting
of celebration in 1867. Some people, perhaps even William Phillips,
regarded this as a public snub to the Lord Lieutenant. Thomas told
the meeting that the Church leaders had suffered a good deal of
reproach for their withdrawal from the procession, but they,

> "did not object to the demonstration itself—none more
> cordially approved of its object, or felt and manifested a more
> sincere respect for the character and position of the late Lord
> Lieutenant and his family, or had greater reason to do so. But
> they could not appear to sanction low and demoralizing
> sports utterly inconsistent with the spirit and purposes of
> Sunday Schools."

Small wonder then that Thomas Thomas was not given a place in
any of the eighteen mourning coaches that made up the funeral
procession of the late Lord Lieutenant in October 1861 *en route* to
the parish church at Trevethin. There were two coach loads of
diocesan and parochial clergy, including the Bishop and Dean of
Llandaff and the Archdeacon of Monmouth with the Vicar of
Trevethin, Thomas Davies. Lords Tredegar and Llanover shelved
their political differences and shared a coach. There were at least two
coach loads of local industrialists ranging from Thomas Brown and
Crawshay Bailey of Ebbw Vale and Nantyglo Iron Works to William
Jenkins and Benjamin Conway of the iron works at Caerleon and
Pontrhydyrun.

The clerics may have been Anglican, but the industrialists were not and several of them were related by marriage to the large family of Conways of Pontrhydyrun, Ponthir and Croesyceiliog, all descendants of the marriage of George Conway and Jane Jenkins of Ponthir in 1775. Thomas Brown's brother James, the Manager of Blaina Ironworks had married Jane Conway, daughter of Joseph, one of George's sons. George's son, Benjamin was at the funeral, alongside his kinsman William Jenkins of Caerleon.

The Chairman at the meeting in Crane Street in 1867, was none other than William Conway then aged forty-seven. When he was nearly seventy, he became the first Chairman of Monmouthshire County Council and was described by his biographer as, "one of the best informed and most reliable politicians of the upper middle class which Monmouthshire ever produced." Allowing for poetic licence in the description of their social status, it has to be said that the Conways constituted a powerful industrial tribe in nineteenth century Monmouthshire, descended from the eleven children of the marriage of George and Jane Conway in 1775.

In three generations, they proliferated over the county causing some confusion by the frequent repetition of the same Christian names and the fact that some of their most prominent members, like William Conway, had no children at all. Not even the redoubtable Sir Joseph Bradney attempted their pedigree. They were staunch Baptists and therefore lacked the benefit of infant baptism, but many of them were buried in the family vault at Pontrhydyrun Baptist Church. William Conway's uncle and namesake had given the land for the building of Pontrhydyrun Baptist Church, and the family claimed by marriage Micah Thomas, Stephen Price, Minister of Abersychan Baptist Church and D. D. Evans, Minister of Pontrhydyrun (*see Appendix*).

Thomas Thomas reminded his audience that day of the first baptism he had conducted on 23 October 1836, in the open air at Trosnant. There had been 242 baptisms since then and others had been admitted to membership from other churches but many had dishonoured their profession and been excluded from the fellowship of the Chapel. The number of active chapel members reached its nineteenth century peak at 197 just before this meeting and the same was true of the Sunday school of 160 with 16 teachers.

The two or three reflections that Thomas Thomas permitted himself in his own speech at that meeting illuminate the character of Crane Street Chapel and the cause of its success as also the success of Nonconformity in the nineteenth century. Aside from the political causes that were espoused, there was the whole attitude towards democratic decision-making in public institutions.

Thomas said that "this Church has always rested on the broad basis of Christian democracy, and has been governed by universal suffrage, including that of the female members. The ballot also has been resorted to on the most important occasions." He instanced the vote on the question of open communion at Crane Street. This was after a request had been made from a communicant who had moved to Pontypool from a Baptist church at Helston in Cornwall, but she had not been baptised as a baptist. The vote of the members was evenly divided at 27 on each side of the decision for open communion and the matter was left in abeyance from 1847, without any attempt being made to change it.

Church officers were always elected by ballot without disturbance "and with perfect freedom of opinion, of speech, and of action." Thomas admitted that there had been in a period of more than 31 years,

> "many differences of opinion, and sometimes collisions of feeling and sharpness of speech, some misapprehensions or offences requiring explanation or forgiveness. But there has never been in office among us a Diotrephes, loving the preeminence, and exercising arbitrary power . . . and there has never sprung up among the people, that root of bitterness, that spirit of selfishness, disaffection, and insubordination, which has caused in some congregation strife, contention, and division."

The allusion to Diotrephes "who likes to put himself first," in the third letter of John, Verse 9, would be wasted on modern congregations but is a reminder of the level of Biblical knowledge in 1867. As the Chapel celebrated their complete payment of the debt owed on the building, Thomas reminded his hearers of its "enlarged operations and extended usefulness in the neighbourhood" and the need for "repairs and enlargement for the free accommodation of the common people, the class who heard the Saviour gladly." Within the next two years, this work was undertaken while the Church met for worship in Tabernacle Baptist Church on the opposite side of Crane Street. It re-opened for worship on Sunday, 11 September 1870.

Crane Street Church, like other Baptist Churches, was organised as a self-governing religious republic with a strict code of Christian faith founded on Biblical doctrine, order and discipline. Thomas had reminded the meeting that the first two members to join the Church from other churches had been excluded from membership for their behaviour. The first, William Wise, was excluded for being one of the Monmouthshire Chartists, ten days after the attack on the Westgate Hotel in November 1839. The second had been excluded for "intemperance, which has been and is the chief bane of our churches." Drunkenness characterised the whole community and parish as commentators such as G. S. Kenrick had observed and it was greater among those who did not attend a church or chapel. Indeed, Kenrick claimed in 1841 that "they (the non-attenders) are all drunkards."

A number were excluded from the fellowship of Crane Street Chapel for "intemperance" but many of the reasons for exclusion were described more generally as "conduct inconsistent with profession" or "immoral conduct" or "immoral behaviour." Other reasons were given as "dishonourable conduct," "long absence from Communion" and even in one case "failure in trade." George Joshua was unanimously excluded on 30 October 1866, because he had been convicted and imprisoned for "dishonest practices." That did not prevent Thomas Thomas from giving his full pastoral support to George's wife, Mary and their six children and even encouraging their son, Caleb to enter the Baptist College in 1874. Caleb became a Baptist minister in 1878 and his two younger brothers, Seth and Frank later became evangelists in South Wales.

In August 1867, the Chapel deacons noted that a number had been absent from Church because they had been working in their public houses "on the Lord's Day." Thomas had always upheld the cause of temperance although there were publicans among the members at Crane Street. In August 1864, the deacons accepted from Thomas the gift of one dozen bottles of Wright's "unfermented" Communion Wine for use at the Lord's Supper.

Most of the members of Crane Street came from local families engaged in trades, small businesses and professional work. In the time of Thomas Thomas's ministry there, the membership included less than a dozen iron and coal miners and their wives, agricultural labourers and gardeners.

In 1868, William Marshall who had been a member of Crane Street since 1849, was crushed to death by a fall in the colliery. He was working alongside his son who narrowly escaped death, but such events were rare for Crane Street where the members were drawn mostly from the middle class or 'shopocracy'. They were designated "gentlemen" by Brynmor Pierce Jones, the historian of the Baptists in Gwent, but that is misleading, not least because the majority of them were female and they were mostly respectable tradespeople who might have been Wesleyan Methodists in England.

They listened patiently to the intelligent expository sermons of Dr Thomas every Sunday. They attended many meetings and midweek prayer groups and lectures, on subjects ranging from the need to repeal the Corn Laws in the 1840s, to the need to abolish Church Rate and liberate religion from state patronage and control. On this subject they were addressed by Mr Edward Miall, MP and Mr John Carvell Williams, Secretary of the Liberation Society.

In September 1862, wide interest was aroused by lectures from Henry Vincent, the old Chartist missionary, on the American Civil War. His sympathy lay with the Northerners because of their desire to obliterate slavery.

In February 1869, Thomas's son, Thomas Henry Thomas (*Arlunydd Penygarn*), delivered a lecture on "Representations of the Saviour in Painting and Sculpture," while a former student of Thomas, Dr Thomas Price of Aberdare, visited Crane Street in September 1870, to give a lecture on the United States of America after his recent visit there on behalf of a missionary society.

Dr Price was used to preaching to great crowds in his Chapel at Aberdare but another of Thomas's former pupils, the Revd Thomas Evans, was a greater crowd-puller at Crane Street when he came on 25 September 1873, to tell the fascinated congregation about "the manners and customs of the Hindoos" (*sic*). Thomas Evans was then a missionary in Allahabad. He had been in India since 1855 when he wrote the first of a long series of letters to his beloved tutor from Calcutta. Evans's first wife had died on the outward voyage but he had married again and had children. His first return visit to Pontypool had been in 1865 after he had survived the privations of the Indian Mutiny including the loss of his house. On his return to India, he had been sent to the Baptist mission at Allahabad and died there as a missionary in 1906.

Eleven

Church Profile

F ROM the membership roll of Crane Street Baptist Chapel, it is possible to identify about 190 active members from its inception until 1871. Apart from the support that Thomas enjoyed from the Conway family and the leadership qualities of William Phillips as senior deacon and Chapel treasurer, a young Pontypool grocer and his wife, John and Mary Havard, became members of Crane Street on 15 November 1840. John was then twenty-three and Mary two years younger. John Havard became a deacon of the Chapel and he succeeded William Phillips as treasurer in 1861.

The Chapel secretary was Thomas B. Smith, headmaster of the British School Pontypool and a member of Crane Street from 29 February 1844. Five years later his wife Ann, school mistress at the same school, became a member of Crane Street. Thomas Brooks Smith also became the Registrar for marriages in Pontypool and so was well known throughout the town.

Thomas and Ann Smith came to Pontypool in 1843 to open the first British School for seventy pupils at Merchants Hill, Pont-newynydd. The school moved to George Street in 1847, but the only assistants to Thomas and Ann Smith until 1871 were monitors trained by them. The school was run on the principles of voluntary-ism advocated by Thomas Thomas as chairman of the committee that had established the school.

The Smiths, who were natives of Horsley in Gloucestershire, were trained to teach at the training college in Borough Road, London. They arrived in Pontypool in their early twenties and remained in their posts until they reached the age of seventy. Their service to the school continued through all its vicissitudes from the voluntary school, which Thomas Thomas visited to check the registers, through British to Board School with a staff of paid teachers after 1871. At least three characteristics of the Smiths were shared by most of the 190 identifiable members of Crane Street Chapel during that period. They were young when they joined the Chapel; they were not born in Pontypool and English was the language they spoke.

Pontypool was a young community where 39% of the population was under the age of fifteen years in the fifty years after 1840. The number of people over the age of sixty-five rose by only one per cent between 1850 and 1875, and by 1891 more than three quarters of the population was under the age of forty. Crane Street Chapel had been built for this young population and it is understandable that most of the members were young especially by the standards of today. About eighty per cent of the members were under forty years of age when they joined the Chapel and many became members by baptism as teenagers.

A number of them became members by letters dimissory from other churches as they moved into Pontypool. Others left the Chapel when they moved away from Pontypool in years of industrial decline. By modern standards, Crane Street Baptist Chapel was overwhelmingly a young church, particularly in the first twenty years of its existence when only three of its members seem to have been over the age of fifty. It was a matter for recording in the Chapel records that on 5 March 1869, "the aged and long—afflicted sister, Elizabeth Henderson, departed this life and entered into rest," at the age of eighty-two. Thirty years earlier at the age of fifty-two, she had been the oldest member enrolled up to that time.

Most of the members, including Elizabeth, also known as Esther Henderson, were born outside Pontypool. Most of those who became members in the first twenty years of the Chapel's life had no birth certificates. Nor were they baptised as infants. Yet it is clear from the records of Crane Street that only about forty of the members were born in Pontypool in the period up to 1871. About sixty-six were born elsewhere in Monmouthshire, with about thirty being born in other Welsh counties. About thirty-five of them had been born in England. Fifteen of the members who joined after 1861 were students of the Baptist College, Pontypool, after a resolution of 29 January of that year permitted all students to be entitled to the privileges of membership of Crane Street Church while they were students of the College. All the students were natives of Welsh counties, including Monmouthshire.

By 1851, one third of the population of Pontypool had been born outside the county of Monmouthshire, and sixty per cent of that third had been born outside Wales. The membership of Crane Street reflected the pattern of Pontypool as a whole in terms of the percentage of its members who had been born in Monmouthshire, but it had slightly more Welsh-born members than was reflected in the population of Pontypool at large. There were still more members who had been born in England.

The language of worship and communication generally at Crane Street was entirely English. By 1860 that was true of almost all the chapels of Pontypool. There was not much sympathy for the Welsh language in Pontypool. Ministers from Welsh-speaking homes who worked hard to acquire proficiency in English so that they could preach effectively, tended to practise their English at every opportunity.

Even Thomas Davies, the Welsh-speaking incumbent of Trevethin, thought that the education of the children of the parish was better served by knowledge of English, although services continued to be conducted in Welsh at St Cadoc's Church, Trevethin until 1891. A commission established by the Bishop of Llandaff, probably under the influence of Lady Llanover, decreed that Thomas Davies's successor as Vicar in 1863 could not be a monoglot Englishman but must be able to speak Welsh. In 1851, more than half the population of the Parish of Trevethin was described as Welsh, but there is no certainty about their ability to speak the language fluently and by 1891 little more than ten per cent of the population of that parish could speak Welsh.

❧

Twelve

Monmouthshire English Baptist Association

THE Monmouthshire Baptist Association (Cymanfa Bedyddwr Mynwy) formed in 1832, clung to the Welsh language. Of the thirty churches in the Association, twenty-two held services in the Welsh language, two were bilingual, Caerleon and Pontrhydyrun, and four were English, including Abersychan. By 1848, there were 55 churches in the Association but there were ten other English churches not affiliated in any way, and by 1866, half the Baptist services in Monmouthshire were conducted in English. With a certain amount of looking over their shoulders, but largely because their young people were increasingly unable to speak Welsh, the Baptist leaders in the county advocated more English churches to meet the needs of English-speaking immigrants to the county.

On 6 May 1857, Thomas Thomas chaired the meeting at Commercial Street Baptist Church, Newport, where services had been conducted in English since 1832. It was agreed to hold a conference at the Baptist College, Pontypool, to consider forming an English Baptist Association of the English Baptist Churches in Monmouthshire and East Glamorganshire. The secretary of the meeting was the Revd Sidney Young of Abergavenny, and the Monmouthshire English Baptist Association was duly formed at the agreed meeting at the College on 21 May 1857; however, the churches of East Glamorganshire never joined. The rules of the Association were drafted at a meeting at Crane Street Chapel chaired by W. W. Phillips on 24 June and the first half-yearly meeting was chaired by Thomas Thomas at Crane Street on 11 November 1857.

After a dinner in the school-room for a large number of people, Thomas Thomas explained that the English people who had moved into Pontypool had spiritual needs "that the Welsh Churches could not meet." He said that an opportunity would be missed and a solemn duty neglected if English places of worship were not provided for the "constant stream of English people that kept flowing in." By 1860 it had become an accepted rule of the Association that "two laymen are chosen for each minister so that the regulation of affairs is more in the hands of members than of the ministers of the churches." It was an underlying principle of the Association, as drafted by Thomas Thomas, that the Association should never interfere "with the complete, separate, independent and individual action of the several churches, except at the request of a properly convened church meeting."

Thomas Thomas was President of the Monmouthshire English Baptist Association on three separate occasions. He was the first President in 1857 and again in 1866 and 1877. On the last two occasions, his presidential addresses were printed as Circular Letters of the Association under the titles respectively of, *The things that are most surely believed among us* and *The Leaven of the modern Pharisees and Sadducees.*

Thirteen

Addresses and Sermons

ADDRESSES

THE circular letter of 1866 was the address that Thomas delivered to the conference of the Monmouthshire English Baptist Association at Crane Street Chapel in April of that year. It was a 'back to basics' appeal to Baptists to realise the essential beliefs that they shared. Thomas reminded them that they shared a common belief in the Bible as "the sole standard of our religion." He said that "the whole Scripture was divinely inspired and profitable for doctrine, for reproof, for correction, for instruction in righteousness." He qualified these remarks by stating that those parts of the Old Testament which were merely civil or political were "abolished by the authority of the Son of God and therefore not binding upon Christians." He said that the Gospel provided the new and better covenant foretold by the prophets. He went on to remind his audience of the great doctrines that were clearly revealed in the New Testament concerning God, the Holy Trinity "whose decrees extend to all the changes of the material creation," and "to all operations of intelligent and moral agents." After referring to the doctrine of the Sovereignty of God, Thomas went on to speak of "those doctrines which are commonly denominated Calvinistic," as he had described them on his application to enter the Baptist College, Abergavenny in September 1822. These were,

> "the sovereign and gracious election of the saved, by God the Father in his beloved son, before the foundation of the world," and, "the fall, depravity and condemnation of all mankind, in consequence of the disobedience of the first man, Adam . . . and the pardon, justification and eternal

redemption of all true believers through the meritorious obedience of the second Adam."

Thomas went on to describe "The particularity of redemption, effectual calling and the final perseverance of the saints," which meant "their certain possession after death of a glorious and everlasting inheritance in heaven; while the wicked, the finally impenitent, are driven away in their wickedness into endless misery and despair." This would be followed by "the second advent of the Lord Jesus, at the end of time and the consummation of all things." This theme is developed in the next chapter.

In the light of the authority of the Bible, Thomas stated his belief in "the holy catholic church," but not "Papists, nor the body of pretentious Episcopalians," but the "general assembly or congregation of the firstborn, whose names are enrolled in heaven . . . the Church for which the Saviour died on the cross," and "beyond the pale of this Church there is indeed no salvation."

The Lord Jesus, said Thomas, is the sole head of this community. There were different classes of officers on earth. The apostles, prophets and evangelists were temporary officers . . . and when they had accomplished their special work, they were withdrawn, and had no successors in office. The permanent officers are the bishops and deacons. "The bishops or overseers of congregations," said Thomas, "are also called elders, pastors, teachers, angels, guides and rulers; and their service relates to the spiritual concerns of the churches."

Deacons were to serve tables and to serve the poor of the flock. Each congregation of,

> "faithful men, making a true Christian Church, have the right and privilege of self-government and free action in the election of its own officers, the admission and exclusion of members, the administration of discipline and the entire management of all its affairs. It justly repudiates the interference of princes and prelates, synods and councils. It submits to no yoke of

bondage, and acknowledges no authority but that of the King of saints, no laws but those contained in the New Testament."

It was the duty and privilege of God's people to support the ministry and the spiritual objects of the church at their own expense. Thomas reminded the members of Baptist churches that too many of them were forgetting their obligation to make financial provision for their ministers.

The only "positive ordinances" of Christianity, he claimed, were Baptism and the Lord's Supper. Baptism for him meant, "the immersion of believers in water, in the name of the Father, the Son and the Holy Ghost: and we can find no authority in the Word of God for the baptism or the sprinkling of infants." The Lord's Supper is,

> "a commemorative ordinance, appointed by Jesus Christ, "to show forth his death till he come . . . but we utterly repudiate the dangerous doctrine of sacramental efficacy, which connects a saving influence with the outward ceremony administered by an authorised ecclesiastic."

He also rejected Confirmation "and the unscriptural forms and notions associated with ordination, matrimony, visitation of the sick, and the burial of the dead." Thomas would have been aware that the service for the Visitation of the Sick in the Book of Common Prayer contained provision for sacramental confession of sins and reconciliation as well as Holy Communion for the sick person. He probably objected to the Prayer Book Office for the Burial of the Dead, because of the committal of the departed "in sure and certain hope of the Resurrection to eternal life." Thomas had probably heard little of requiem Eucharists in the Church of England at that time. Had he done so he would have been horrified. He believed that nothing done by the living could affect the state of the departed.

Most Anglicans would have agreed with him. Whereas Catholic Anglicans like Roman Catholics would have prayed for the dead and some Anglican priests would have celebrated requiem eucharists, Evangelicals would have suspected a return to the doctrine of Purgatory with masses for the departed to free them from the pains of Purgatory. At the heart of the Reformation was the doctrine of Justification by grace through faith in the merits of Jesus Christ and not through any works that might be performed by ourselves or any priest on our behalf. In 1898, Archbishop Frederick Temple decreed that prayers for the dead were lawful in the Church of England.

Thomas's readers were again reminded that *civil* government is ordained by God and all civic officers and leaders must be obeyed "in secular affairs." If civic leaders interfered with religious convictions and forms of worship, they could not expect obedience which belonged only to God. By the same token, God had decreed the observation of the Sabbath Day, which had become the first day of the week for Christians as "the Lord's Day," on which he rose from the dead, and its rightful observance had the authority of the Apostles and the first Christians. Thomas deplored the profanation of this day for business and pleasure. At the same time he rejected all the festivals and fasts "appointed by a carnal priesthood, and observed by the Churches of Rome and England."

Thomas concluded his Circular Letter of 1866 with an exhortation to all baptised Christians to imitate Christ's example and exhibit his virtues. Just over a decade later in a circular letter that was his last published work, *The Leaven* of *the modern Pharisees and Sadducees* (1877), Thomas detected that the leaven of the ancient Sadducees was working through the popular literature and periodicals which were impregnated with scepticism and lack of faith. Men of high scientific attainment had failed to "look through nature to nature's God" and so they had become lost in the mazes of philosophical speculation. People should have faith in God and believe in our Lord Jesus Christ.

The Churches also needed to beware of the hypocrisy of the Pharisees which substitutes the shadow for the substance or power of godliness. In particular Thomas condemned "the revived spirit of ecclesiastical ritualism." He did not refer to the Anglo-Catholic ceremonies then appearing in Wales, but he went on to condemn the Roman Catholic Church as "little else than christened pagan-ism," and said that the Anglican Church "united to the state in this country, is but Popery modified and reformed; but still retaining much of its heathenish ceremonialism, and some of its most unscrip-tural doctrines" such as infant baptism. He condemned the doctrine of baptismal regeneration "as absurd and heathenish as the Hindoos' (*sic*) purification from sin by ablution in the river Ganges."

The Anglican Book of Common Prayer taught the doctrine of regeneration. Immediately after the priest had baptised the infant and received him into the Church, he said "Seeing now . . . that this child is regenerate and grafted into the body of Christ's Church." The baptised child was thus born again by baptism as a beginning of new life in Christ. God had taken the initiative and the act of faith had been made by the parents and godparents. Baptists believed that the candidate for baptism had to be able to make the act of faith in Jesus Christ for himself and be born again after repentance and total immersion in the waters of baptism. Not-withstanding the Judgement of the Privy Council in 1850 in favour of the Anglican Evangelical view that regeneration was conditional upon the subsequent faith of the baptised infant, the differences between Baptists and Anglicans seem to lie somewhere between the perception of God's grace in the sacrament and the extent to which that grace depends upon the faith of the recipient.

He then went on to denigrate the "Churching of women," the thanksgiving in Church by mothers for their safe delivery from childbirth, as probably an imitation of the Jewish rites of purifica-tion of women after childbirth under the law of Moses. Confirmation he condemned as "a doctrine and commandment of men, and has no foundation in Holy Scripture . . . and its utter vanity is manifest in the thoughtless, irreligious, and wicked lives of most of those who have submitted to it."

He denied to marriage the status of a sacrament, describing it as "a civil and domestic institution." He urged gratitude for "the law which recognises the civil nature of the matrimonial union and leaves all to add any religious services they may deem proper without the interference of the state priest." Thomas hailed the Lord's Supper as "a real sacrament" but he denied transubstantiation, the sacrifice of the mass, the description of the holy table as an "altar" and the kneeling posture to receive Holy Communion. He entirely rejected "the ritualistic and sacerdotal notions with which the sacrament of the Lord's Supper has been invested."

It was to be expected then that he would condemn "the constitution of a human priesthood" as "anti-Christian," because the New Testament knew nothing of priesthood except that of "the Great High Priest over the house of God." The whole body of Christian believers formed "a royal priesthood," said Thomas, "but the impious assumptions of the Romish hierarchy are reflected by the Protestant priesthood in England and Wales."

He went on to condemn the sacraments of the Holy Eucharist and Holy Orders and Penance as practised by the Anglican Church. "It is in the highest degree presumptuous," thought Thomas,

> "for ordinary ministers to assume what clearly belonged to the Apostles and other inspired men. Also to pretend by imposition of their hands and other formalities, to invest their successors with spiritual authority and power, of the reality of which they can furnish no evidence . . . Sacerdotalism . . . has still great power, and its surroundings are very imposing and captivating to many minds. Clerical vestments, crosses and candles, floral decorations, architectural symbols and pictorial representations, all addressed to the eye rather than the heart, to sense rather than conscience, are developments of the ritualistic spirit and aids to sacerdotal pretensions. Let us therefore, firmly repudiate all priestly assumptions, and maintain the permanent offices of pastors and deacons in their simplicity and purity as described in the New Testament."

Thomas concluded this letter with another condemnation of "the feasts, fasts and vigils, with which the religion of our land is encumbered." They might be very agreeable to "our sensuous and depraved nature" but the New Testament set apart only the Lord's Day as "obligatory on Christians." He condemned the keeping of holy days and quoted St Paul's Letter to the Galatians, Chapter 4, Verses 9-11, against their observance. Thomas claimed that dissent was not quite free from the ritualism of the State Church. He urged all Baptists to "repudiate human authority in matters of religion and the Pharisaism which makes void the law of God." They should acknowledge the Lord Jesus Christ as the sole Head of the Church, and His revealed will as their only rule of faith and practice.

SERMONS

Thomas Thomas has been accused of writing 'purple passages' in his published pamphlets. However, Thomas Morgan of Skewen, a Baptist Minister who had known Thomas and wrote a short biography of him in 1924, claimed that Thomas's sermons, delivered mostly from notes rather than scripts, were models of measured and graceful delivery and expository style. Thomas had a gift for clear and simple exposition. His manner was sincere and unaffected and his sermons were delivered without oratory. Although Welsh was his first language and his very last sermons were delivered in Welsh, Thomas more often preached in English because that is how he believed he was best understood.

His sermons were based on Biblical theology and were full of Biblical quotations. Morgan illustrates this from the notes of Thomas's sermon on the, "duties of Church Members to their Pastor":

1. Recognise the Divine Institution of the Pastoral Office. Ephesians IV. Luke X:2

2. Render due submission to the authority of the Pastor. Names denote some kind of authority. Rule not arbitrary or legislative, 1 Peter v, 2 and 3. But due submission to the

law of Christ, Hebrews XIII, 7-17. 1 Thessalonians V, 12 and 13.

3. Pray for them. Apostles needed the prayers of the Church. How much more uninspired ministers? Acts IV 29. XII 5. Romans XV.30 Ephesians VI 19. Colossians IV.3. 2 Thessalonians III 1.

4. Render them liberal support. 1 Corinthians IX, 6-18. 2 Corinthians XI 7, 9.

5. Co-operation with your pastor as far as possible. Deacons, members, females: Phoebe, Priscilla. Romans XVI 2,3,4,9. Philippians IV.3.

Contemporaries did not regard Thomas's sermons as too academic but he was a teacher and his method was expository. One contemporary, quoted by Morgan, claimed that, "his sermons were massive in structure, orderly in arrangement, and the appeal they made was usually based upon a reasoned statement of truth."

Thomas was always in demand as a preacher on special occasions like chapel anniversaries or at the opening or re-opening of chapels, as he did at Pontrhydyrun Baptist Church on 16 August 1837, and at every special service of that Church for the next fifty-four years until a fortnight before he died. He preached at the re-opening of Horeb Baptist Chapel, Blaenavon on 14 March 1863. He preached many ordination sermons for students of Pontypool Baptist College and the students remembered them. One former student, Revd Thomas Lewis of Newport, later a Baptist historian, remembered the three questions that Thomas put to him at his ordination at Llanddewi Rhydderch in 1848:

> What proofs have you that you are a true Christian?
> What proofs have you that you are called to the Ministry?
> What are the doctrines you believe and intend to preach and defend in your public ministry?

When the two churches, Crane Street, Pontypool and Zion, Trosnant, Pontypool were amalgamated on 7 July 1878, Thomas preached two sermons and "administered the ordinance of the Lord's Supper" in the evening for about a hundred members from both churches. Soon after that event, Thomas noted that he had preached 7,381 sermons since April 1821 and more than 5,000 sermons since he had settled in Pontypool in 1836.

The verdict of Morgan, his biographer, on Thomas as a preacher was that "he was a good Biblical scholar and his knowledge of the Bible was amazing." Most tellingly, Morgan claimed that Thomas was "one of the last group of Puritans, and if those noble characters knew anything, they knew their Bibles."

Thomas's preaching was Christo-centric and Crucifixion-centred. He was a pacifist who preached more often in the cause of peace than suited everyone's tastes. He was also remembered for preaching against the Established Church, but his best arguments against the Church of England were reserved for his speeches that were later published as penny pamphlets.

Fourteen

Disestablishmentarianism

THE establishment of the Church of England as the State Church of England and Wales, was organised in the two Provinces of Canterbury and York. This was an arrangement brought about by the English Reformation under Henry VIII and his son Edward VI, and settled by his daughter Elizabeth, after a brief interlude while the country returned to Rome under Queen Mary. Elizabeth became Supreme Governor of the Church of England and her successors inherited the title. The Elizabethan Settlement of religion had never achieved its intended comprehensiveness because Puritans (later called Presbyterians, Independents and Baptists), as well as Roman Catholics were excluded by successive Acts of Parliament. As the Settlement depended upon Parliament's statute law for its enforcement, so the right to dissent from the Settlement also depended upon parliamentary statutes.

Only by Act of Parliament were Protestant dissenters granted freedom of worship under the Toleration Act of 1689 and the right to hold public office through the repeal of the Test and Corporation Acts of 1828, although there had been annual indemnity acts since 1727. The Roman Catholic Emancipation Act of 1829 granted the same freedom to Roman Catholic subjects.

That dissenters sought redress of their grievances through Parliament would seem to be a cause of little surprise except to some Anglican historians who seem shocked by the politicising process of the disestablishment campaign after 1844, when the British Anti-State Church Association, later known as the Liberation Society, was formed. Thomas Thomas with his friends and colleagues at Pontypool had formed an active branch of the Association from its earliest days. Decades before there was even a Member of Parliament for Pontypool, let alone a secret ballot, Thomas and his friends believed that it was only Parliament that could free Nonconformists from the control of the State Church and advance their cause by removing their civil disabilities.

In 1965, Canon E. T. Davies, the doyen of Welsh Church historians, in an important study of *Religion in the Industrial Revolution in South Wales*, condemned the Baptists for their political attitudes towards industrial society in the nineteenth century. Davies acknowledges that the English Baptist Association showed more concern for the social needs of the industrial areas of Monmouthshire than the Welsh Baptist Association. He still contrasts the rejoicing of the Baptist Association in 1834 "that the Act for the abolition of Negro slavery would soon come into operation," with the "indifference to those social problems which affected thousands of their members in this industrial society." Yet at the same time, he asserts that "more than any other denomination in these industrial areas, the Baptists did not hesitate to reveal clearly their allegiance to the Liberal Party." Such allegiance was surely understandable and contradicts Davies's point about their indifference to social evils since they believed that only by voting Liberal could the problems of their industrial society be resolved.

In the case of Thomas Thomas, the criticism is unfair because his manifest sympathy and support for the cause of the poor in industrial society has already been indicated by his words at the time of the agitation for the repeal of the Corn Laws. Thomas influenced Baptist contemporaries far more than Davies perhaps realised, but more of that later.

The difference between Anglicans and Baptists is perhaps nowhere better exemplified than in their attitude towards what happened in 1662. For the loyal Anglican, this year marked the Book of Common Prayer enforced by the Act of Uniformity after the Restoration of the Monarchy under Charles II. The nineteenth century Baptist associated that year with the betrayal of Nonconformists through the failure of Charles II to honour the Declaration of Breda. This was followed by the hated Clarendon Code as a result of which 1,760 Puritan Ministers were ejected from their livings in the Church of England and lost their livelihoods.

Davies noted the "general Nonconformist celebration of the Act of Uniformity which was held in Swansea on 23 and 24 September, 1862." This was really a conference of the Liberation Society, described by another Welsh historian, Kenneth O. Morgan, as "a massive meeting at Swansea called to commemorate the 'martyrs' expelled under the Clarendon Code in 1662." Edward Miall and J. Carvell Williams were prominent, but also present were Henry Richard, Dr Thomas Price of Aberdare, Stephen Price of Abersychan, a couple of the Conways and Dr Thomas Thomas. These were among 128 Ministers and laymen who participated in the conference.

In a conference to explore how Welsh Nonconformists might play a more prominent part in government because of their increased numbers and their importance in the Liberal Party, it was Thomas Thomas and Thomas Price who stole the political thunder from the Independents, as Davies observed. Davies approved of the sensible speech of Thomas Price, who pointed out that Wales did not have enough Nonconformist leaders of ability and independent means to become Members of Parliament at that time.

By contrast, Thomas Thomas was castigated by Davies for his "fine exhibition of demagogy in a paper he read on, 'the importance of developing the power of Welsh Nonconformity,' for the liberation of Religion from State patronage and control," and for his purple passages in a paper described as "interesting" by the *Cambrian* newspaper of 26 September 1862.

At that time, the Church in Wales as later constituted, did not exist and the country of Wales, merely "a geographical expression," according to one Bishop of St David's, was organised as four dioceses of the Province of Canterbury. Until 1881, with the passing of the Sunday Closing (Wales) Act, which did not then apply to

Monmouthshire, no separate legislation was made for Wales. Yet what Thomas Thomas proposed in 1862, when much of Wales was not even interested, was separate treatment for Wales in the matter of disestablishment from State control of the Church because the number of dissenters in Wales was overwhelmingly greater than the number of Church people.

Thomas's basic premises about disestablishment were simple. Civil government had no right to determine the religion of its subjects. Thomas expressed disappointment that the Protestant Reformation in Europe did not sever the Church from the State.

He said that the clear aim of the Liberation Society was to secure,

> "the unconditional abolition of Church Rates, the right of sepulture in parochial burial-grounds, the entire removal of religious tests from the national universities, the abolition of the Maynooth endowment and the Irish Regium Donum, the release of the Bishops from the House of Lords, the resumption by the State for secular purposes of the tithes and other public property, with due regard to existing claims and interests, and the cessation of all authoritative interference on the part of the Crown and the Government with the officers, the maintenance, the disciplining and the worship of any religious body."

Thomas went on to remind his audience that the Liberation Society "invokes the earnest co-operation of Welsh Nonconformity; and I am anxious to impress this conference and the public mind with the vast importance of employing the power of the dissenting body in this great enterprise."

Christians in every country are citizens who have civil rights and duties, Thomas argued. He believed that church establishments were contrary to Holy Scripture because the Jewish theocracy could not be imitated by earthly rulers, or be a model for a system of government founded on human laws. Under the Emperor Constantine, the pagan priesthood was replaced by a Christian priesthood and nominal Christianity became allied with the secular power, but this had curtailed the liberty of Christians and changed the whole character of the Christian Church.

The purple passage to which E. T. Davies took exception soon followed:

> "It (the Established Church) adds to the crimes of past ages a dogged resistance to the reforming spirit of the present time; fills the highest offices in the Establishment with nominees of Government; monopolises charitable trusts; insists on the indelibility of "holy orders;" upholds intolerant laws, not excepting the iniquitous and ensnaring Act of Uniformity and clings to ecclesiastical abuses of every kind. It seizes four or five million pounds worth a year of national property which it lavishes upon dignitaries and palaces, while thousands of useful labourers have barely the necessaries of life; and very many are thankful for small doles of charity or gifts of old clothes. It perverts for sectarian purposes the educational grants of Parliament, fights for Church Rates and disdains not the crumbs of Easter offerings, while it insults the feelings, seizes the property and sometimes imprisons the persons of conscientious Nonconformists."

Canon E. T. Davies did not like the tone of Thomas's remarks, but if this is a 'purple passage', it states clearly what Thomas found objectionable about the Established Church of England and why he thought that the Church, for which he had no personal spite, would be better off without the shackles of State control. "The Episcopal Church here (in Wales) would lose by the change nothing worth retaining, but would probably gain immensely in purity, simplicity, and usefulness," he said. But he had still not reached his most important paragraph in relation to his theme:

> "Look now, at Wales. What has the Establishment done for religion or our people, which would not have been much better done without it? . . . We say, look at poor Wales, with less than half the population of London, scattered

over thirteen counties and behold the thousands of chapels, ministers and schools, with colleges and missions, all created and sustained by Christian willinghood, not only without State aid, but with the disadvantages of the proximity and opposition of the endowed Church."

That was the burden of Thomas's message. He believed that the task of civil government was to liberate the churches to preach the Gospel and preserve the voluntary principle. This required Liberal members of Parliament to be elected throughout Wales to bring about the disestablishment of the Church here.

Dissenters should "qualify and register!" In the meantime, Nonconformists should offer much more passive resistance or active disobedience to Church Rates. Church periodicals should assist with the necessary publicity in bi-lingual editions and the tracts of the Liberation Society should be translated into Welsh.

There was no doubt about the weight of Thomas's contribution to the arguments of a conference that clearly anticipated what would happen in the General Election of 1868, when Liberal representation would be increased in Wales and Henry Richard was returned as the Member of Parliament for Merthyr Tydfil.

Thomas's criticism of the Established Church never prevented him from working closely with Anglican colleagues, such as the Vicar of Trevethin or the Rector of Panteg, on causes of mutual interest such as the Scripture Readers' Association in Pontypool or the Pontymoile Working Men's Institute. Thomas addressed the annual meeting there in April 1859, presided over by William W. Phillips, in the presence of the Revd Thomas Davies, Vicar of Trevethin, and the Revd Dr David James, Rector of Panteg, on the benefits to be derived from Mechanics' Institutes.

All three men were Welsh-speaking, but Dr James was a more ardent Welshman than either Thomas or Davies.

Thomas attended the funeral of Thomas Davies, Vicar of Trevethin, on 8 May 1863, and he expressed his high opinion of

Dr David James at a public meeting in Crane Street Chapel in November 1859, when Thomas was asked to chair a Liberation Society meeting there. The *Pontypool Free Press* reported that Thomas insisted that he had no intention of undermining the work of the Church of England. He said that those who sought dis-establishment did not assume an attitude of hostility to any Christian denomination or church. He said that "one denomination of Christians had been taken into the patronage of the state . . . and peculiar privileges were conferred upon this one denomination, to the entire exclusion of the rest." He went on to remind the meeting that some of them had heard the Revd Dr James telling a meeting a few days earlier that he was not free to work publicly outside his own parish of Panteg, whereas Dr Thomas was at liberty to go wherever he liked.

This meant that there were limits to the parochialism of the Church of England but "a man of eloquence and learning, such as Dr James, ought not to be confined within the narrow limits of a parish, but be allowed to travel through the length and breadth of the land."

As far as Thomas's direct support for Liberal Party candidates at general elections was concerned, he actually proposed Mr Edward Capel Whitehurst as a Liberal candidate in opposition to Colonel Poulett Somerset, the Tory candidate for the County seat in Mon-mouthshire that had been held by his family since 1805. After service in the Crimean War, Poulett George Henry Somerset was prepared to succeed his cousin Edward Arthur Somerset as one of the two MPs for the County of Monmouthshire.

The other County seat was held by the Morgans of Tredegar House, and Thomas thought that the time had come to support a candidate who best represented the views of the majority of the electors even in 1859. In proposing Mr Whitehurst, Thomas had first to overcome the opposition of "a clerical-looking gentleman," who "challenged Mr Thomas's right as an elector, a question which was set at rest by the Rev gentleman handing his card to the sheriff," according to the account in the *Pontypool Free Press*.

Thomas agreed that Poulett Somerset would faithfully and honourably represent the ducal house of Beaufort, but he did not think that he possessed any qualification to represent the large constituency of Monmouthshire because he was simply the nominee of the house of Beaufort (cheers and uproar), and the views he put forth were not such as might be expected from an enlightened gentleman in the second part of the nineteenth century (uproar).

They were antiquated views, they were what might be called antediluvian notions (great laughter and uproar), they did not belong to this age, or properly this country. Thomas said that the Colonel had told them that he was warmly attached to "the glorious principles of the Reformation." These principles, said Thomas, were, liberty and judgement in all matters of religion, no domination of one party over another on account of religious views, and no man could maintain those principles who upheld the imposition of Church Rates.

That did not prevent the election of Poulett Somerset on that occasion and also in the two subsequent elections of 1865 and 1868. In the campaigning for that election, Thomas addressed a crowded meeting at Pontypool Town Hall on behalf of the Liberal Party candidate, Colonel Henry Morgan-Clifford on 17 September 1868, as he had already at Abersychan on 26 August. He said that he was prepared to do everything he could for the Colonel because he had felt for many years that it was a great disadvantage that the county should be misrepresented by two gentlemen who, however estimable they might be in private life, were entirely disqualified for representing the county of Monmouth. (Hear, hear).

In the event, Colonel Clifford, who had served as MP for Hereford between 1847 and 1865, received 2338 votes compared with 3525 votes for Poulett Somerset and 3761 votes for C. O. S. Morgan of Tredegar Park. At that election, so fruitful for increased Liberal support in Wales, Thomas also spoke on behalf of the Liberal candidate in Brecon. He knew that Nonconformists would not be heard until they had Members of Parliament who heard their cry.

Part Four

THE WISDOM OF AGE
1870-1881

Fifteen

Presidency of the Baptist Union

O N 12 January 1870, Thomas celebrated his sixty-fifth birthday. He continued to be pastor of Crane Street Church where the membership was in decline from its peak of 197 in 1865 towards the figure of 135 in 1873. That was when Thomas made his decision to resign as minister to concentrate upon his work as President and theological tutor at the Baptist College. He felt guilty about his inability to visit as many members of Crane Street Church as he would have liked or to spend as much time in sermon preparation as he wished, but he was still an effective leader of the Church. At the time of Thomas's birthday, the congregation of Crane Street was meeting for worship at the Tabernacle Baptist Church opposite because the Chapel building was being renovated and enlarged by the addition of two side galleries. A building committee headed by Dr Thomas and William Conway, met regularly to plan the campaign to raise the thousand pounds that were spent over fifteen months and to oversee the extensions. The Chapel re-opened on 11 September 1870, and plans were made to revive the Sunday School, where the number of people attending had declined to 120 with twelve teachers, from the 1867 figure of 160 with sixteen teachers. T. B. Smith, the Sunday School Superintendent, also became the Secretary of the Church in January 1871.

Communion tickets were introduced at Crane Street on 12 November 1871, presumably to monitor those who were entitled to make their communions. Thomas continued to provide the wine for Holy Communion, which was unfermented and remained so after his retirement, though the communicants did not have indi-

Dr Thomas Thomas, 1805-1881

vidual communion cups during Thomas's time as pastor. Nor did the Chapel have a grand pipe-organ as central feature, but only a simple harmonium for accompaniment.

In 1872, Thomas was elected President of the Baptist Union of Great Britain and Ireland. This was the greatest honour that could be bestowed on a Baptist Minister and Thomas was the first Welsh-speaking Welshman to receive it. Thomas said that he was conscious of his great age of sixty-seven when he was elected and he spoke of his unworthiness to hold such an important office. Perhaps it was his sense of unworthiness in worldly terms that caused Thomas to speak in his inaugural address to the annual meeting of the Union in London in April, of the unworldly character of the Christian religion and its evangelical theocracy. In his address, Thomas gave thanks for the large measure of civil and religious liberty that Baptists then enjoyed. He said that worldly pursuits detracted from religious worship and practice. Love of money was a distraction as were frivolous amusements, certain light reading, dissipating entertainments and the wrong friends. He condemned the wasting of money on personal adornment, costly furniture and useless decorations and elegancies, "and often a corresponding parsimony in the support of Christian objects at home and abroad."

When Thomas came to consider his subject in relation to the normal services of worship in Baptist Churches, he thought that the evangelical theocracy was not best served by regarding all Baptist services as public worship; this was because Nonconformists repudiated the principle of a national establishment. As a Puritan, Thomas believed that Baptists should not make an effort to appeal to worldly minds in their acts of worship. Baptist Churches were in danger of simply copying the national Church by recognising as Christians, people whose lives showed no evidence of conversion. Such people were simply attenders rather than worshippers. Through the encouragement of prayer-leaders by the pastors of Churches, the intellectual and spiritual power of the Church fellowship could be developed. The arrangements of services demanded serious and prayerful consideration and too much should not be left to the pastor alone.

None of that trenchant criticism provoked any reaction from Thomas's hearers, but his next point proved to be very contro-versial, when he came on to consider the unworldly character of Christianity in relation to millenarian speculations. In a world that has just celebrated the second millennium with technological foreboding that was not realised, millennium speculations may do more to confuse than enlighten. To Thomas Thomas and his Church, millennium speculations meant the return of Jesus Christ in glory as Christians confess in the Creed. The millennium in that context related to the thousand year reign of Jesus Christ at the end of this world and the establishment of his Kingdom on earth. The question in dispute between some Christians in Thomas's time was whether Jesus would come again suddenly in a cataclysmic way to start the millennium (premillennialism) or whether he would come again at the end of a golden age when the world was ready for his Kingdom (postmillennialism).

Thomas was clear that the teaching of Scripture about the end of the world is that there would be one general Resurrection and not two, and after that the Judgement. What passed at that time as 'millenarian theory' could not, said Thomas be reconciled with the plain truths of Scripture. The theory which became known as pre-millenarianism was that Jesus would come again from Heaven and set up his throne at Jerusalem, when the tribes of Israel and Judah were settled in their ancient possessions. Jerusalem would be a seat of universal empire and Jesus would reign there for a thousand years "over glorified saints and martyrs and myriads of mortal men." The priesthood would be reorganised in the restored city where the temple would be rebuilt on its ancient site, and sacrifices and offerings again be offered to God.

Thomas thought that the possible return of the Jews to Palestine and their remaining a separate people or becoming spiritual members of the Body of Christ, had no necessary connection with a pre-millennial advent and the personal reign of Christ on earth. Thomas did not know what is now known about Zionism and the appeal of this pre-millenarian theory to so many Zionist Christians today. He stood simply upon the evidence of Scripture that Jesus must sit at his Father's right hand until all his enemies, including death, the last enemy, have been destroyed. He will raise up believers at the last day, not before. Pre-millenarianism, with its worldly grandeur and military power, was something that Thomas thought contrary to the biblical teaching of the kingdom which grows from small seeds like the mustard plant and is a spiritual dispensation, the new and everlasting covenant of grace. Thomas believed that pre-millenarianism undervalued the great commission to preach the Gospel to every creature and denigrated Christian missions as a waste of time. There is, he said, no hint in Scripture that the "spiritual dispensation" of the kingdom is to be superseded by an economy of, "worldly grandeur, military power and cardinal ordinances in incongruous alliance with the heavenly and divine." Such a retrograde movement would not be in harmony with "the progressive development of divine operations," from the time of Creation until the coming of Jesus.

He criticised the literal interpretation of the prophet Ezekiel's vision of the temple, priesthood and services as "absurd and its realisation physically impossible."

Most importantly, Thomas regarded all this pre-millennial speculation as incompatible with the spiritual reality of the Christian faith. Thus the preaching of the Gospel to the whole world, the work of Christian missions and the translation and distribution of the Scriptures, would be a waste of time, money and effort because all this could be achieved by the coming of Christ to reign on earth for a thousand years. What need was there for a Gospel of reconciliation or the fulfilment of the "great commission" of St Matthew, 28: 18-20?

Thomas's own belief about the second coming of Christ was very much under the heading of post-millennialism. There would be a second coming of Jesus, but it would be more gradual and less cataclysmic than the event envisaged by pre-millenniarists. Jesus would come again in glory at the end of the age. This event would be assisted by the ministry of reconciliation and through the out-pouring of the Holy Spirit. There would be peace on earth. God's kingdom would come "and God's will be done by men on earth as by the angels in heaven." This was the prevailing view held by theologians in Britain and America in 1872, but there were still theologians on both sides of the Atlantic who held the pre-millenniarist viewpoint, as Thomas was soon to be informed.

By the early twentieth century Thomas's post-millennarian position had largely disappeared among evangelicals because its optimistic viewpoint about the trickle-down effects of "the temporal benefits connected with the Messiah's reign," had acquired a secular character. Thomas's view of its outcome had been otherwise. He thought the prospect most inspiring to spiritually-minded people because "it encourages prayer and stimulates exertion in the whole Church."

After dealing with the millennium, Thomas went on to view the unworldly character of the Christian religion as it affected the question of national education. On this subject, Thomas acknowledged that he differed from many of his fellow-Baptists, but his opinions were "the deep-seated convictions of my inmost soul." He admitted that his opinion on the subject had not changed for a quarter of a century. He remained totally opposed to government interference with popular education. In defence of his opinions, Thomas quoted Dr Richard Winter Hamilton's "Crosby Hall Lectures," and other authorities, including Edward Miall and Henry Richard who "proved the high state of morality and religion to which the Welsh people had attained without State aid." He also quoted J. H. Hinton and the resolutions of the Baptist Union at Norwich in June 1847, which described the use of public money to pay schoolmasters as "nothing short of its application to religious instruction," and "the essential principle of national religious establishments." Thomas reiterated the principle avowed by the Baptist Union in 1843, "that the education of the community is not the proper business of the State," and therefore education should be free from government interference.

In his support, he quoted the Congregational Union and other organisations who had declared that education was not a function of government. If it is, said Thomas, then teachers of religion in church, chapel or Sunday school will have to be treated in the same way. If moral and religious truth is an essential element of true education "then it must be beyond the province of civil government; and all interference with it must not only be a violation of the fundamental principle of Dissent, but also an invasion of the Kingdom of Christ." Nonconformists, he claimed, had been forced under such circumstances to support the demand for a system of secular education.

It was a fallacy to think that it was the duty of the government to educate the nation. Moreover, said Thomas, it was a fallacy to assume that the government was competent to educate the nation or fit to be a moral teacher because it patronised demoralising customs and amusements such as war and the liquor trade. Thomas went on for more than half his published address of twenty-four pages, to denigrate the government's system of public education and its poor results in terms of the continuing ignorance and illiteracy of the people and the failure to produce "the general enlightenment, morality, and religion of nations."

Thomas was certainly no believer in the value of state education to improve morals, manners and responsibility towards society. People's practical intelligence and moral worth could not be assessed by their school-learning, he said.

On the contrary, there were thousands who were unable to read and yet they lived virtuous lives and "tens of thousands who, like the common people of the Principality of Wales, have learnt to read the Book of God and other useful works, and who faithfully discharge their domestic and social duties. Many of them cannot write their own names, but they know their God, their Redeemer and their duties, and are exemplary members of society," because, said Thomas, there were influences at work "above those of the school and the professional teacher."

The chief fallacy about education, thought Thomas, was that ignorance was the cause of crime and crime could be eliminated by education. There was no evidence for this and knowledge, while good, did not of itself produce virtuous lives. Thomas cited well-educated criminals from all countries as far apart as France and the United States, England and China, from ancient Rome to modern Germany. From these he concluded that, "crime is the attendant of knowledge as well as of ignorance."

To discover the real causes of crime and the best ways of solving them was important to Thomas. He was convinced, after spending forty-four years as a pastor in London and Wales, that the main cause of crime was drunkenness. The Clergy, the judiciary and the police, he said, were all agreed about this, but the government's answer was Forster's Education Act of 1870, which, "caused bitter disappointment to the friends of religious freedom, imperilled the stability of the government, alienated the advanced Liberals, roused the great body of Nonconformists to take a position of determined antagonism, and filled the land with agitation, conflict and alarm."

Forster's Act sounded the death-knell of voluntaryism in education. Gladstone would have welcomed a degree of voluntaryism, by permitting religious denominations to supply the religious teaching in the Board schools according to popular demand, but Forster proposed non-denominational teaching. For voluntaryists like Thomas Thomas, the whole principle of state-funded education with teachers appointed by the state and a system of government inspection of schools, not only favoured the establishment, but set up what he described as "an educational State Church," where "the Vice-President (W. E. Forster) stands for the Metropolitan of all England, Inspectors for Lord Bishops, trained and certificated teachers for priests and deacons, and government grants and local exactions for tithes and Church-rates."

Thomas was continuing a theme he had taken up in a letter to the *Nonconformist* newspaper as long ago as 16 December 1854, when he expressed his continuing support for voluntary education and his opposition to state educationists. In that letter, Thomas said that, "it would be quite as consistent with the fundamental principle of dissent for the tutors of our colleges, and the pastors of our

Churches, to receive their salaries from the government, as it is for the teachers of the British schools to do so for their services in imparting to the young the great truths and precepts of Christianity." He also referred to the headquarters of the British and Foreign Schools Society in Borough Road, Islewood, as "the educational Church establishment in the Borough Road."

Thomas regretted that the principle of voluntaryism had been sacrificed on the altar of state-funded education for people who were willing to provide education for themselves.

He condemned Nonconformists who had departed from the principle of the voluntary system by accepting government grants for the maintenance of British schools and so allowing the state to interfere with voluntary education. This all harked back to Thomas's disputes with William Roberts over such grants in the twelve years after 1853. Roberts died two months after Thomas's address.

Thomas also distrusted the nature of non-denominational (secular) education. He said that it could not be unsectarian, but it would be no concern of the churches as he saw it, because the Church's task lay elsewhere. Yet Christians were bound to promote the religious education of all the people "and the duty becomes the more urgent in proportion as secular instruction is spread abroad among all classes." He thought that Baptists should give more attention than ever to their parental duties, to Sunday schools, to Bible-classes, to Biblical lectures, to collegiate institutions, and to home and foreign missions. Pastors and teachers should preach the Word of Life more earnestly and effectively, "not only in our comfortable chapels but in school rooms and halls, in fairs and markets, in streets and large towns . . . and in every convenient place."

As leader of the Tories, Disraeli claimed that Forster's Education Act established "a new sacerdotal class of schoolmasters," clearly reflecting the thoughts of Thomas Thomas on the subject. Had Disraeli, who had famously, 'caught the Whigs bathing and made off with their clothes' in 1867, been listening to the arguments of the voluntaryists? Or was Thomas Thomas, for once in his life, 'on the side of the angels'?

At a time when presidential addresses of the Baptist Union were receiving increasing attention, and in spite of all the time devoted to his views on education, the only section of Thomas's published address that caused any controversy consisted of the four-and-a-half of the twenty-four pages that he devoted to "Millenarian specu-lation."

A pamphlet of thirty-one pages was published containing the observations made in a lecture at Wellington Hall, Islington, London, in reply to Thomas's millenarian opinions. The observations were made by someone described simply as "a former member of the Baptist denomination who still believes in the ordinance of Immersion." The holder of the pre-millennial belief criticised by Thomas had realised that this view had been held by Baptists at an earlier period and particularly in America at the beginning of the nineteenth century.

Thomas's critic took him to task about his interpretation of Old Testament prophecy and his theology of the Kingdom of God. Thomas believed that the Kingdom was present in Jesus Christ and through him in the hearts of believers. The Kingdom is thus past and present. Thomas's critic was a fundamentalist in the interpre-tation of the prophetic books of the Old Testament. The critic believed that the Kingdom of Christ could only come in the future according to a strict interpretation of the vision of "the stone cut out of the mountain without hands" (Daniel 2:45) which referred, said the critic, to an event after the establishment of Christianity.

In response to Thomas's teaching about the spiritual nature of Christ's kingdom or rule as a spiritual state, the critic claimed that it was only in this world that Christ's kingdom could be located and it was in the land of Canaan that the promised kingdom would be set up. The doubt that Thomas cast upon the return of the Jews to Palestine as a subject of prophecy under the Divine Providence was condemned by the critic as "an extraordinary position . . . for one who professes to be a master in spiritual Israel." The critic quoted a prophecy of Jeremiah (Chapter 3:18 and 30:3) to demonstrate that, "in those days the house of Judah shall walk with the house of Israel . . . to the land that I have given them for an inheritance unto your fathers . . . and I will cause them to return to the land that I gave their fathers, and they shall possess it," but there is no indication here of date or time, any more than there is in relation to the prophecy of Ezekiel 37:21 and 22, that he quotes in the same way.

Modern readers, who know the reality of the State of Israel, may wonder when we can expect the reign of Christ to begin. The critic went even further because (s)he was a 'Christian Zionist' determined to assert that the New Testament predictions about the significance of Jesus's birth foretold, for example by St Luke, Chapter 1;31-33, could only be fulfilled by the return of Jesus to the throne of David in Jerusalem to "reign over the house of Jacob for ever"(Luke 1:33).

The critic took Thomas to task for saying that "the literal interpretation of parts, at least, of Ezekiel's vision of the temple, priesthood, and services, is absurd, and its realisation physically impossible." Likewise, Thomas's suggestion that it would be impossible for "all the nations of the earth to gather to the feasts at Jerusalem," is answered by the suggestion that "only a portion of a nation need be present at one time." Clearly Thomas's critic was more literalistic about the Bible than he was. There is also a clear difference in the understanding of prophecy and the time-scale of prophetic fulfilment.

To some extent the critic misses the main point of Thomas's theme which was that the Kingdom was not of this world but was spiritual. To encourage the fulfilment of millenarian hopes and apocalyptic in a literalistic way, so that the kingdom was projected as an earthly state under a Jewish state-controlled hierarchy, was to create the nightmare against which Thomas fought for every waking hour of his ministry. With no sense of irony, Thomas's critic assures his readers that the God of surprises will provide *a posteriori* what could never have been envisaged *a priori*, as he always has. This particular surprise, he claims, is well-documented in Old Testament prophecies even if they were clearly written for a different audience on a different time-scale. It must also seem strange to Christians, as Thomas observed that the fulfilment of Christian hope should be understood as the restoration of an earthly Jewish temple in which animal sacrifices would be offered to God and these sacrifices would supersede the Christian worship that replaced them.

Thomas read this anonymous criticism to which he responded briefly in his second presidential address to the Baptist Union in Manchester on 10 October 1872. "Some remarks in my former address have elicited a number of friendly private communications from unknown brethren; and my observations, more especially on the millennial reign of Christ, have called forth several elaborate answers in the press. This I do not regret. No harm can come from honest discussion, conducted in a proper spirit."

Thomas went on to say that he only wanted to give honest and open expression to his own views on the subject without any wish to provoke acrimonious dispute about issues on which people could agree to differ. He apologised if he had wounded anybody's feelings or caused harm to the Baptist Union. In that spirit of unity and reconciliation he went on to discuss the subject of the Baptists and Christian Union.

Thomas began by praising the unity that had been achieved among the Baptist churches by the Baptist Union in the previous fifty years. The evidence of greater co-operation was most conspicuous in Wales where there had previously been strife caused by Pelagianism (denying God's grace), Arianism (denying Christ's divinity), and Socinianism (denying the Trinity). Division had also been caused about the need for imposition of hands at the time of ordination and the place of singing in public worship. There had been hyper-Calvinism (predestination to eternal life and to damnation), and Fullerism (the teachings of Andrew Fuller, 1754-1815, moderate Calvinism, free will, universal atonement) which influenced Micah Thomas and Christmas Evans. North Wales had been much influenced by Alexander Campbell, 1788-1866, who was very concerned about the imminent second coming of Christ as well as baptism by immersion. Before Campbell, Baptists in North Wales had been impressed by Robert Sandeman, 1718-1771, a Scot who rejected the idea of a State Church, regarded faith as "mere intellectual belief" and tried to return to primitive Christianity in belief and practice, celebrating the Lord's Supper every Lord's Day and holding love-feasts and feet-washings.

The love-feasts were meals shared by members of the church at Sunday lunchtimes after they had been to Holy Communion. The feet-washings were in imitation of what Jesus did for his disciples at the Last Supper. Many churches do this today on Maundy Thursday, but the Sandemanians did it every week.

Sandemanianism never had huge numbers of followers but its supporters included the physicist, Michael Faraday as well as Christmas Evans who described how he was under "a black cloud" of Sandemanianism in North Wales between 1795-1802.

By 1872, Thomas believed that the Baptist denomination was moderate Calvinist. It was not anti-Evangelical, but accepted in substance the views of Andrew Fuller. From Cardiff to Holyhead and from Monmouth to Milford, Baptist churches belonged to a county or district association. He went on to survey the development of the Baptist colleges in Wales, from that in Pontypool, increased from eight students in 1836 to thirty-six in one particular session, to the colleges in Haverfordwest, founded in 1839, and Llangollen, founded in 1862. Each college employed two tutors to teach about fifty students between them. There was a growing conviction, said Thomas, that the Welsh churches could not support three colleges efficiently. Better training could be achieved by one college with four or five tutors teaching fifty or sixty students with better entrance qualifications. He thought that many of them by preparing for external degrees of London University could be better prepared for the demands of the age in which they lived.

In 1872, it seemed to Thomas that the Baptist churches were closer together theologically than they had been throughout the eighteenth and early nineteenth centuries. They all seemed to accept moderate Calvinism. Some differences remained about the necessity and use of Baptism, the Christian Ministry, feasts of love, the kiss of charity and feet-washing.

There were more serious disagreements about the terms of communion, State education, the nature of the Millennium, the second advent of Christ, the final end of the world, and the doom of the wicked. However Particular (Calvinistic) and General (Arminian) Baptists could co-operate together more closely and more frequently, as had been suggested in 1864 by the Chairman of the Baptist Union, Revd J. P. Mursell. This was, observed Thomas, because, "General Baptist Churches are quite accustomed to choose Particular Baptist pastors; and a proportionate, but not an equal number of General Baptist pastors are settled over Particular Baptist Churches." General and Particular Baptists frequently exchanged pulpits and the same sermon seemed equally acceptable in both places. There was thus, in Thomas's mind, no obstacle to the union of those two sections of Baptists. That union was eventually achieved in 1891.

Thomas did not live to see that outcome, but he was not content to leave matters there in 1872. After one body of Baptist Churches had been formed, he urged his fellow Baptists to consider closely "the practicality of a closer union with other evangelical denominations." To a considerable extent he believed that friendly relations already existed between Baptists, Independents, Wesleyans, Presbyterians, Primitive Methodists and others. They exchanged pulpits, gave mutual service and co-operated for the public good. He thought they could even unite with pious members of the Established Church, "though they were the adherents of a system from which we and our fathers have suffered untold wrongs."

Thomas welcomed the scholarly co-operation of Biblical translators from all the churches, Baptist and other Nonconformists, as well as scholars of the Church of England, who were working to produce the Revised Version of the Bible. Thomas took a keen interest in this work. He lived long enough to read the Revised Version of the New Testament in May 1881, but not that of the whole Bible in May 1885. He described the work as,

> "a greatly improved version of the oracles of God, and must convince all thoughtful persons, however prejudiced, in circles most remote from Nonconformity, that there are rich stores of wisdom and erudition to be found apart from mitres and cathedrals, peerages and palaces."

Modern evangelicals should note that Thomas did not share their devotion to the "authorised version of King James," which in his view owed some of its blemishes "to the exclusive Episcopalianism and royal dictation."

Thomas did not believe that the time had come in 1872, if it ever would, for an undenominational organisation of all Christians, but he saw a greater readiness to co-operate and to contribute towards the prayer of Jesus, "that they all may be one . . ." (John 17:21).

He claimed, in the concluding part of his address, that the Baptist Union embodied and disseminated principles of philanthropy which would ultimately unite the whole human family. Baptists from all over the world preached the Gospel throughout the world. Baptists were among the foremost of those who promoted the abolition of slavery in the United States of America.

Baptists were second to none except the Society of Friends, in advocating international peace, so that,

> "there is without doubt, a deepening and spreading conviction in the popular mind that war is a game which, were their subjects wise, kings would not play at; and that it is better to decide disputes before the sword is drawn than after human blood has been shed."

He thanked the Liberal Government for preserving the world from the calamity of a European war and settling the differences with the United States by a Court of International Arbitration. These were references to the way in which Gladstone had kept Britain out of the Franco-Prussian war in 1870 and achieved a settlement on the Alabama dispute, thus ending a century of strained relation with the United States in 1872. It was fitting that Thomas's last address to the Baptist Union should end on the subject of peace about which he had prayed and preached so much during his ministry.

Sixteen

Preparations for Retirement

IN October 1872, Thomas was still pastor of Crane Street Church as well as being President of the Baptist College. By 1873, it was clear to the members of Crane Street that their beloved pastor intended to retire soon to concentrate for his last few years of active ministry upon the work at the College. On 23 February 1873, they presented him with an address 'numerously signed' in which they urged him to reconsider his decision and requested him to continue. They promised him "more general co-operation" because they were conscious of their failure to make their own contributions to the ministry of the Church. Thomas delayed his final decision until 2 September 1873, when he told them that he would be resigning as their pastor at the forthcoming Christmas.

A committee of professional and businessmen met under the leadership of the Classical Tutor at the College, W. Mortimer Lewis together with William Conway and John Havard, Chapel deacon, treasurer and grocer, and others, to plan the farewell presentation for Dr Thomas. A committee of ladies, consisting of their wives and daughters, Mrs Havard and Miss Havard, Mrs Smith, Mrs Fowler, Mrs Wayman, Mrs Lewis, butcher, Mrs Davies, Tŷ Mawr, Mrs Dauncey, Mrs Eckersley, Miss Conway, Miss Sheppard, Miss Bevan and others, met to plan a presentation to Mrs Thomas and decide who was going to make the tea.

The life of the Chapel continued as normal. On 26 October 1873, John Havard informed the Church meeting of the death of John Miles, the miller of Trosnant, aged seventy-four, who had been

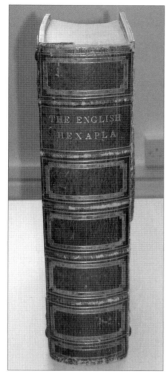

one of the first members of the Chapel in 1838. John's wife Margaret was very ill and short of money, and she was given one pound and ten shillings from the Church's poor fund.

In November, the men's committee decided to present Thomas with an illu-minated address, but this was changed to a silver mounted Hexapla as selected by Thomas himself, with an engraved silver plate inserted. This was a book containing the Greek New Testament with six English translations in parallel, vertical columns. It was decided to present a testimonial to Mrs Thomas.

On Sunday, 10 December 1873, Thomas celebrated the Lord's Supper at Crane Street for the last time as its pastor.

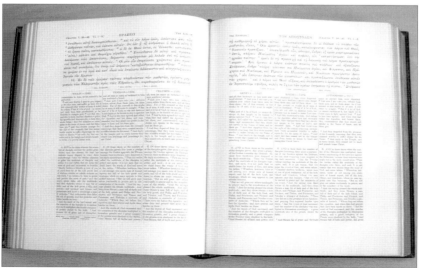

Silver mounted Hexapla containing six English translations
of the Greek New Testament
(Courtesy, South Wales Baptist College, Cardiff)

A larger number than usual attended. On 28 December he preached his last sermon as Pastor on the text of 2 Timothy 4:6, 7 and 8. He had indeed fought the good fight and kept the faith.

On 29 January 1874, at a tea at five o'clock for about 150 members at Crane Street, John Havard presented Thomas with a purse containing one hundred guineas and Mr Peter Eckersley, a local merchant, presented the "beautifully silver-mounted English Hexapla containing the original Greek of the New Testament with six English versions at different times." As described by the contemporary account the book was adorned with a silver shield and an appropriate inscription and a magnificent cushion was given by Miss Florence Dauncey.

The Ladies' Committee presented Mrs Thomas with "a very handsome time-piece bearing a suitable inscription," but Mrs Thomas was too unwell to attend the presentation and Thomas responded to her presentation as well as his own. The Church minutes record that he presented her sincere thanks for the gift and he alluded to "her good qualities as a wife and to the very material aid she had ever afforded him in enabling him to discharge his arduous duties." Had she responded to her own presentation, she would have been the only female speaker that day. There were no female deacons at Crane Street before 1918, and women were not normally expected to speak in Church at that time. Speeches were made by Mr John Bevan, the secretary of the Presentation Committee, the Revd Stephen Price of Abersychan, a life-long friend, Mr Joseph Goodenough, a deacon, and the Revd W. M. Lewis. "Thus ended," says the official record, "one of the most affecting and deeply interesting meetings ever held under the roof of Crane Street Chapel."

Three years after resigning as pastor of Crane Street Church, Thomas retired from the presidency of the Baptist College at Pontypool. He announced his resignation to take effect at the end of December 1876, but he and his wife did not move into their retirement home at 45, The Walk, Cardiff until June 1877. Thomas's successor, as President, W. Mortimer Lewis, was in very poor health,

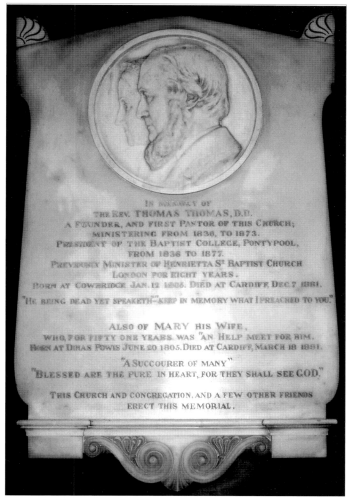

Marble memorial tablet in Crane Street Baptist Chapel
of Thomas and Mary Thomas

and his term of office proved to be almost as short as that of Thomas's successor at Crane Street, Revd C. R. Page, who resigned on 21 April 1878.

The grand presentation to Thomas on his retirement from the College was made at the Tabernacle Baptist Church, The Hayes, Cardiff, on 20 September 1876 and reported in the *South Wales Daily News*. This was the Church to which Thomas had belonged

*Retirement home of Thomas and Mary Thomas
at 45 The Walk, Cardiff*

as a boy and where he had preached at the age of fifteen. The large
meeting at Tabernacle for his retirement was presided over by the
Right Hon. Sir Robert Lush, Q.C., a famous Baptist lawyer who
had known Thomas since his days at Henrietta Street Baptist
Church, London. Sir Robert spoke highly of Thomas's work at
Pontypool, where between 500 and 600 students had been trained
for the Baptist ministry, though he recalled the regret he had felt at
Thomas's departure from London so long before.

After a number of friends and former students had spoken in
praise of Thomas, Sir Robert called upon the Revd Dr J. W. Todd

of London, an old student and friend of Thomas, to make the presentation which Todd had initiated. The presentation consisted of an illuminated address together with a purse containing no less than two thousand guineas. The Mayor of Cardiff attended as well as Dr Hugh Jones, the president of Llangollen Baptist College, Revd William Edwards, Thomas's former student and eventual successor who took the College to Cardiff, and numerous clerical and lay colleagues as well as members of Thomas's own family, including his son, Thomas H. Thomas (*Arlunydd Penygarn*), who illuminated the address.

The Revd Charles Stovel of London, President of the Baptist Union ten years before Thomas and his fellow-student from Stepney days, spoke of the esteem in which Thomas was held by his fellow-students. Efforts were then being made, Stovel recalled, to "resist the much abhorred African slave trade" (Applause).

In the debates at Stepney College about the slave trade, Stovel had found "Dr Thomas, firm in principle, kind in heart, and pure

The home of the South Wales Baptist College, 52-58 Richmond Road, Cardiff

in motive . . . in his opposition to slavery and in the essential principle of separating the Church from the State . . ." (Applause). Stovel said that he had been firm as a rock and a great source of encouragement. Stovel went on to reveal an essential feature of Thomas's character that while he was "marvellously pacific—kindness seemed to be his nature—his movements and thoughts seemed to prepare the way for difficult and important things."

After two more speeches from fellow clergymen, Dr Todd read a letter from the Revd Charles Spurgeon, nearly thirty years younger than Thomas but the leading evangelical preacher in London. Spurgeon regretted that he had never met Thomas, but said that he held him in high regard. Dr Todd then read aloud the address, engrossed upon vellum "in beautifully illuminated characters."

The address told the tale of Thomas's life. It recorded that he had left his London pastorate forty years earlier to become president and professor of theology at Pontypool.

The College had prospered under Thomas because,

> "by your native endowments and various attainments and Christian culture as well as by your unswerving faithfulness to duty, and unobtrusive devotion to God alike in spirit and in life, you have inspired and moulded the characters of hundreds who have accounted it their joy to sit at your feet, elevated the tone and character of the Baptist Ministers in Wales, and placed the Churches of our denomination in wider regions under lasting indebtedness for the pastors you have educated and matured."

The generous gift of 2,000 guineas had been donated by Baptists from "England, Ireland, Scotland, Wales, Africa and both Indies." Thomas thanked the Chairman, Sir Robert Lush for presiding and making the presentation together with Lady Lush.

He commended Sir Robert because "in the upright Judge we recognise a brother and a friend, who everywhere holds fast his

Christian profession, and is not ashamed of the principles of the members of the Baptist denomination." He also thanked Dr Todd for initiating the presentation and also the local secretaries and treasurers. He was surprised by the great generosity shown to him by his friends and also the large contributions of many old students who, in spite of very limited means had given subscriptions. He was sincerely grateful for a donation that would enable him and Mrs Thomas to live far more comfortably in retirement than would otherwise have been the case. "No doubt," Thomas reflected truthfully, "I would have been a better pastor if I had not been a tutor and a better tutor if I had not been a pastor. But I have done the best I could under the circumstances." Thomas quoted St Paul, "By the grace of God I am what I am" (*Trwy Ras Duw yr ydwyf yr hyn ydwyf*) as shown at the bottom of the illuminated address.

Thomas then recounted the principal events of his life, his birth in Cowbridge, the farm at Leckwith Bridge, the clergyman's school he attended at Llandaff and William Jones's school in Cardiff. He recalled how he first attended Baptist meetings at the Star and Garter public house near Cardiff Castle following his conversation with two of his father's farm labourers.

He recalled that after his baptism in the River Taff in his thirteenth year, he became a member of the Church at the Star and Garter and an assistant to William Jones at the school. He entered Abergavenny Academy in 1822 and went on to Stepney Academy two years later. In 1828 he became Minister of Henrietta Street Church, Brunswick Square and he preached frequently in the open air at Farringdon Market and Somers Town on Sunday mornings.

With the hindsight of forty years, Thomas thought that the eight years of his pastorate in London had been the happiest years of his life. The membership of the Church had increased from forty to one hundred and fifty or more and he and Charles Stovel worked together for five years as secretaries of the Baptist Building Fund. He said that he had taken a special interest in Welsh cases and was able to help them.

He recalled his surprise at being invited to succeed Micah Thomas as President of the College that moved to Pontypool and was connected with the English congregation there. "I accepted the call, and incurred the needful sacrifice and risk, trusting in the Lord and the goodwill of Welsh ministers and Churches." At one time the students at the College had reached the extraordinary number of 36. He praised his erstwhile colleagues, Revd George Thomas, "a man of massive intellect, sound learning, and most amiable disposition, with whom I worked in unbroken harmony and affection for 30 years," He also praised James Sully and W. M. Lewis, who had raised standards in the Classical Department so that several students had taken external London University degrees. Thomas described the enlargement of the College in his time and the payment of the debt of seven thousand pounds. He thanked the College committee and the House committee for looking after the internal government of the institution.

He ended by thanking his wife for her management of domestic affairs and for "her cheerful and self-denying service of a true help-meet, whose prudence and gentleness, forbearance and firmness, entitle her to a large share of the honour conferred on her husband; and who through long years of affliction, darkened with the shadow which the death of four beloved ones long since left upon her gentle spirit, is still the unobtrusive but guiding and controlling power of the collegiate household."

Thomas said that he hoped to retain his interest in the College a little longer, and he finished with a prayer that God would continue to sustain him in his old age.

A large party then went to lunch at the Town Hall with the Mayor of Cardiff, where further speeches were made. The grand scale of this occasion as well as the full printed report of the proceedings indicates the important place that Thomas had come to hold in society at that time.

Seventeen

Retirement and Death

IN June 1877, Thomas and Mary Thomas moved to 45, The Walk, in the Parish of St John's Cardiff, where they had been married. They lived not far from Richmond Road, where Pontypool Baptist College would follow in 1893. Thomas and Mary settled into their large retirement home with Mary's niece, Ann David. They celebrated their Golden Wedding anniversary on 23 February 1880, with a public gathering at the hall of Bethany Baptist Church, Cardiff. They received a congratulatory address from Crane Street Church.

Thomas went on preaching, praying and reading throughout his retirement. He remained a keen student of the New Testament and continued to read both Greek and Latin. Mary Thomas died at 45, The Walk, on 18 March 1881 at the age of seventy-five. She was buried in the burial ground at Penygarn Chapel, Pontypool, where her two sons, Llewellyn and William had been buried as well as her niece, Anne Henry.

Thomas went on preaching until the end of his life. On 20 November 1881, he preached one of the sermons at the re-opening (again) of Pontrhydyrun Baptist Chapel. On the following Sunday he preached at Llantwit Major and on Tuesday, 29 November he attended the Central Committee of Pontypool College, where the 'infantile' behaviour on the part of some immature students was becoming a cause of concern to Thomas's successors. His last two sermons were preached in Welsh, on Sunday, 4 December at the Tabernacle Chapel, Pontypridd. Appropriately, his last sermon was preached from the fifth chapter of Revelation, "And the four living creatures said, 'Amen'." This great song of praise to God reaching its

Tabernacle Baptist Chapel, Penygarn

climax in Amen, "so be it", was a very fitting conclusion to the thousands of sermons that Thomas had preached and to his whole life's work.

Thomas died of a stroke in his sleep on Wednesday, 7 December 1881, a month before his seventy-seventh birthday. His only surviving son, Thomas Henry Thomas was then living with him, but it was his faithful niece, Ann David, who discovered him. Thomas Henry inherited 45, The Walk, and all the other possessions bequeathed by Thomas in his will of 30 November 1866, to his wife Mary, who had predeceased him. T. H. Thomas, the artist, was then well-known in Cardiff in his own right. He was already a widower since the death of his wife, Ellen Sully Thomas, a sister of Thomas's former colleague at Pontypool. Ellen had died in childbirth at 45, The Walk, in 1879 at the age of forty-four and the child had been still-born. This final tragedy in the lives of Thomas and Mary Thomas deprived them not only of their daughter-in-law, but of all hope of grandchildren and direct descendants.

In his will of 30 November, 1866, Thomas requested that his remains be buried with those of his children in the vault at Penygarn, "and that my funeral be open and public but entirely free from all pomp and display and . . . that no mourning whatever be given to any persons except near relatives in attendance."

Thomas's funeral began at seven o'clock on the morning of 12 December with a special service at Tredegarville Chapel, Cardiff, conducted by the Minister, the Revd A. Tilly. The Revd J. P. Bellingham, formerly of Pontypool, and the Revd Nathaniel Thomas, a former student of Pontypool College, both spoke. After the service, a procession went to Thomas's home and accompanied the hearse as far as Roath Court Funeral Home on the Newport Road. There

Thomas Henry Thomas (Arlunydd Penygarn)
Artist, Author and Naturalist, 1839-1915

were said to be a thousand people in the procession, including several Baptist choirs who sang hymns *en route.*

The hearse and cars then continued by road to Crane Street and other relatives and friends travelled by rail to Pontypool. The Chapel at Crane Street was full. The coffin was placed on a black-draped stand in front of the platform-pulpit. Thomas's son and his two brothers, William and John, were there as well as many other mourners including William Conway, William Edwards, Dr Thomas Price and Dr Rowlands, Llanelli.

The service started with a reading from the Revd John Williams, Minister of Crane Street. The Revd A. Tilly then offered a prayer thanking God that Thomas had been spared much illness, but had been taken in the fullness of his life. A long address was delivered by the Revd Dr Todd in which he referred to Thomas's life, character and work: "This elegant Church in which we are assembled is the fruit of his untiring labours, as are also not a few on earth and before the Throne who, within its walls, were touched by his eloquent appeals, and turned their heart unto God."

There followed addresses from the Revd Evan Thomas of Newport, who had entered Pontypool College as a student in 1842, and had become a renowned preacher, the Revd Dr Davies, President of Haverfordwest College, the Revd J. W. Lance of Newport and the Revd Dr Roberts of Pontypridd. After them came the Revd William Edwards, Principal of Pontypool College, Revd N. Thomas, who spoke in Welsh, Revd S. R. Young of Abergavenny and the Revd Dr Price of Aberdare who said that the happiest years of his life were spent at the College, "and during those years, I found in Dr Thomas, a model man in all senses of the word." A Welsh hymn to the tune 'Dorcas' was sung. It had been arranged by T. B. Smith, still at Crane Street, and the organ was played by his daughter. The Revd Thomas Lewis of Risca, another old student, offered a prayer at the grave in Penygarn. The funeral was fully reported by the *South Wales Daily News* on 13 December 1881, and also by the *Pontypool Free Press* on 16 December.

Part Five

EPILOGUE

Eighteen

Principles, Leadership and Contribution

WHAT sort of person was Thomas Thomas? To describe him as a Welsh Baptist Minister in South Wales in the mid-nineteenth century is to invite stereotype and to forget that his major contribution was made as the first Principal of the Baptist College at Penygarn, Pontypool for forty years. The time and the place were both important for the development of his character and his thinking. Pontypool was an old industrial town, the oldest in Monmouthshire. The county might not have been regarded as Welsh, and there might still be Welsh people and Welsh historians who have their doubts, but Pontypool's pedigree was impeccably Welsh when Thomas arrived there in 1836.

As a Welsh-speaking Welshman, he did not have to apologise for realising that the town, like the rest of industrial south-east Wales, was changing under the pressure of successive waves of English-speaking immigrant workers. The communication of the Gospel and the future of his own denomination depended upon the ability to preach and teach effectively in the English language. Students applying to enter Bristol Baptist College to train for the ministry had been rejected because of their poor command of English. Thomas's task was to teach his students to communicate in English.

He spearheaded the foundation of the Monmouthshire English Baptist Association. He was its first president in 1857 and on two subsequent occasions in 1866 and 1877. During that time the Association increased from eleven churches with 610 members to thirty-two churches with 3,121 members.

Yet he was the first person to declare publicly, as President of the Baptist Union of Great Britain and Ireland, that there should be much closer union between the associations and sections of the Baptist Church, whether general or particular, and even with the other evangelical denominations. Thomas, like other Baptists, might respect the independent democratic government of the local congregation, but he rejoiced in the co-operation and fellowships of Baptist associations and evangelical fellowships for the achieving of their common purposes.

Thomas never worked in isolation. He was highly regarded by his colleagues in every aspect of his ministry. His strong-minded judgements meant that he usually emerged as the leader wherever he was, but it was a calm, eirenic leadership in spite of his firm principles. Thomas Thomas was a puritan. In terms of the classical Puritanism of the past, he could never have accepted the principle of a State Church established by law according to the religion of the Sovereign.

The one thing he regretted about the Reformation was its inability to detach itself from such a compromise and in terms of the demands of the Puritans, to effect a full and true Reformation that extended the principle of the authority of Holy Scripture, as described in Article Six of the Thirty-nine Articles. In true Puritan terms, Thomas believed that what was not commanded in the Bible for faith and worship was forbidden. The Bible was the main source of his preaching and his prayers. Sabbatarianism held sway. The Lord's Day was the Christian Sabbath and the day devoted to worship. There might be week-day prayer meeting and lectures, but only on Sunday was it necessary to worship God in Church and red-letter saints' days or even festivals that did not fall on Sunday could be ignored. That applied even to Christmas Day.

As a puritan, Thomas had no great love of the theatre or popular entertainment or dancing or church bazaars. His reaction to games in the park for Sunday Schools has been recorded as well as his antipathy to smoking and his abhorrence of alcohol. He and his family and his extended family of students at Penygarn lived very simply and frugally. In his personal behaviour and relationships, Thomas was very straightforward. From his writings and his biographer Thomas Morgan, it is clear that Thomas meant what he said. His word was his bond. Such a simple style is attractive not only because it is rare nowadays but because its integrity reflects the Sermon on the Mount, "Let your word be 'Yes, Yes' or 'No, No'; anything more than this comes from the evil one" (Matthew 5:37).

Thomas had a great love of music which he had been taught to read and sing as a child. He had none of the Puritan objections to hymn-singing, but his deafness precluded much of it for himself in later life and Crane Street had only a simple harmonium for accompaniment in his day. There were no outward sacred symbols such as the Cross or stained glass windows or even the large pipe organ of later days. At the same time, Crane Street Chapel was no white-washed Bethel with plain interior in cottage or farmhouse style. As stated earlier, it was a magnificent classical temple, designed by J. H. Langdon with fine portico and strong interior design with an engraved glass roof.

Charles Spurgeon would hardly have approved. It suited the middle-class congregation it served in an important town of shop-keepers. They paid for it but the platform-pulpit and the glass roof were Thomas's idea.

What might be identified as evangelical spirituality in Britain at the time when Thomas came to Pontypool, had originated in the Evangelical revival of the eighteenth century, associated in Wales with the names of Howell Harris, Daniel Rowland and William Williams, Pantycelyn. This spiritually affected all the larger dissenting denominations, Baptists and Independents as well as the Methodists. It also influenced a large number of parishes in the Established Church in England and Wales. As the diocese of Llandaff began to come alive under the influence of Bishop Ollivant after 1850, the Church became more involved in the social life of its communities. As Wilton D. Wills has observed, "What is remarkable about the 1850s, is the sensitivity of all the religious denominations to the problems of the new and rapidly expanding society, and the close harmony and co-operation between the denominations in solving these problems." Religion in the South Wales Coalfield during these years was essentially 'social' and non-doctrinal. The dominant feature of Victorian evangelicalism was a strong desire to improve society, 'to build Jerusalem', which produced in the Coalfield a remarkable ecumenical spirit . . ." The high-water mark was the religious revival and temperance movement of 1857-61. Wilton D. Wills describes the period 1850-70 in the diocese of Llandaff as "one of 'low-Churchmanship, in which the character of Anglicanism, particularly in the Coalfield, came to resemble that of Nonconformity" with more varied forms of services in which the sermon was the climax and the audience participated through hymn-singing.

Evangelicals placed great emphasis upon the awakening of the individual conscience to the need of forgiveness and a consciousness of salvation through faith in Jesus Christ by the grace of God. The doctrine of the Atonement was central to Evangelical theology and individual conversion was the most important requirement of Evangelical spirituality; hence the emphasis upon preaching and the centrality of the pulpit with its open Bible in evangelical Churches. Individual scriptural holiness and an awareness of personal salvation were the aims of evangelical preaching. The emphasis upon the individual conscience by evangelicals resulted in an encouragement of much practical philanthropy and the involvement of evangelicals in practical political programmes and movements of emancipation after the example of Wilberforce in his fight against the slave trade. Certainly, Thomas Thomas's own opposition to slavery and his campaigns for social justice on behalf of the poor and the disenfranchised in his own society were evidence of a similar social conscience developed by evangelical concern.

In spite of the particular position of the Baptists about Baptism of adult believers by immersion and their opposition to the Baptism of infants, which provoked some notable dramatic performances in South Wales in mid-century, there was general evangelical agreement upon many social and spiritual needs. Thomas Thomas had very good working relationships with Independent colleagues like Evan Jones (Ieuan Gwynedd) and Thomas Bright in the debates over education, as well as with Edward Miall and others in the Liberation Society. Indeed, the career of Samuel Roberts (S.R.), of Llanbrynmair, an Independent minister in North Wales and an exact contemporary, revealed the same social concerns as Thomas over the abolition of slavery, voluntary education, the Anti-Corn Law League, the temperance movement and the cause of pacifism.

Although there was much common ground with Anglicans through a shared evangelical theology, the obstacles to co-operation with Anglicans were caused by the civil disabilities under which Nonconformists lived. The halcyon days of 1857-61 were still bedevilled by the campaign against Church Rate, no burial for Nonconformists in the Churchyards on which they had paid the rate and no right of admission to the universities of Oxford and Cambridge. So however much historians like Wilton D. Wills might see the years 1857-61 as a period of harmony and common purpose between the Christian denominations in South Wales, the worm of discontent was always turning on the issue of state patronage and control of religion.

In 1859 in Pontypool, Thomas Thomas stood shoulder to shoulder with his Anglican colleagues, Thomas Davies, the much-respected Vicar of Trevethin and Dr David James, the scholarly Rector of Panteg. This occurred at the annual meeting of Pontymoile Working Men's Institute at the Hanbury Arms in April and the annual meeting of the Scripture Readers' Association at the Town Hall in November. Nothing stronger than tea was drunk at the former when Thomas extolled the virtues of Mechanics' Institutes, and he "resumed his seat amid great applause" at the latter after he had advocated the importance of the Scripture Readers' Association of which the Vicar of Trevethin was the local secretary. Many Anglicans also attended when Thomas presided over the large public meeting of the South Wales Total Abstinence Association in the market place in Newport in September 1859.

All these social concerns were important to Thomas and he was a recognised leader at all those meetings. He valued the co-operation of Anglican colleagues, but he still pressed on with his support for the Liberation Society. He chaired the meeting of the Society at Pontypool in November 1859 when he claimed that disestablishment would be a benefit to the Church of England as well as to Nonconformists because it would give all Christians greater freedom to worship and work together.

That meeting of the Liberation Society was most concerned with the abolition of Church Rate, but Thomas used the opportunity to echo what he had said in his lecture of 1847, that the ultimate object of evangelical Nonconformists was "the liberation of religion from its bondage to the State, and the consequent euthanasy of dissent." Euthanasy was an early alternative word for euthanasia to describe a quiet death.

The sentence expresses a rare sentiment at that stage in the development of disestablishmentarianism. When the struggle reached its climax and disestablishment was achieved in Wales, the sores on both sides were such as to prevent the positive progress in cooperation among the churches for many years. In the words of R. Tudur Jones, a great Congregationalist historian, the long battle for disestablishment was "a major disaster. If the Nonconformists had come to delight in hostile language, the Church had become hardened by obstinacy . . ." For Thomas it was a fundamental principle that there should be no interference by the state in the religion of the people. He believed in the polity of Baptist churches as self-governing republics with pastors, teachers, elders and deacons after the pattern of the New Testament, and the democratic vote of the members of the local church was the last word in the government of that church. Thomas avoided at least two caricatures that can arise in such circumstances. He was never ruled by his deacons, but he was often the peacemaker and arbitrator when strong-minded deacons disagreed.

Such was the case in 1871 when John Havard as treasurer and Thomas B. Smith as Chapel secretary, quarrelled over the kind of event that Thomas Thomas hated and knew would cause disagreement. This was a bazaar held in the Town Hall in September in aid of the building fund which benefited by more than £170 from the bazaar. Thomas helped the two deacons to resolve their disagreement by 26 November. In that respect, Thomas was greatly missed after his resignation from Crane Street. His successor was short-lived and John Havard resigned from his post and joined another chapel.

Thomas also avoided being the person who did everything at Crane Street. His dual role as principal and pastor made delegation necessary, but he had always taught the principle of collective pastoral care with teams of visitors and deacons who investigated matters of concern to the fellowship of the church. As President of the Baptist Union, Thomas had urged Baptist ministers to select suitable people to read lessons and to lead prayers in the local churches for the development of lay spiritual leadership.

The voluntary association of those who had covenanted together for the worship of God was the pattern of association that Thomas wanted to extend to schools. The government should have no more control of schools and their syllabuses than they did in churches. Thomas was one of a strong group of voluntaryists in the Pontypool area, but according to Nefydd, he was the ringleader and the inspiration behind the opposition to government grants for British schools that cost the County of Monmouthshire so dear in terms of religious education for Nonconformists in their own schools. The National schools of the Church of England proliferated while the Nonconformist schools remained unbuilt.

In Thomas's mind the principle was consistent with no government interference in the religion of the people because that would only introduce the prejudices of the Established Church through the system of government inspection. Thomas would have preferred the American system, which kept all religious teaching out of the schools. There may be many today who still regret the way in which the funding and philosophy of education have become a political football to be kicked around for the benefit of those who see schools as means to political ends. At the same time, there were no winners in the Nonconformist determination to keep schools as doctrinally-free zones in the teaching of the Christian faith.

When the Board schools were introduced after 1870 to fill the gaps left by the refusal of the voluntaryists to sponsor British schools, the insistence upon non-denominational Bible-teaching produced a situation that satisfied neither Nonconformists nor Anglicans and eventually resulted in a faithless secularism in county schools. That was far from being the intention of Thomas Thomas, whose vision was for locally-financed schools where religious education could be under the direction of the local churches. That was a vision shared by Gladstone in 1870, but one which was never realised in county schools.

By 1870, at the age of sixty-five, Thomas Thomas was four years older than Gladstone. His thinking had been formed on a number of important issues at an earlier period in his life. One of his heroes, Robert Hall, a great Baptist preacher who died in 1831, had preached an important sermon at Bristol in 1820, condemning what Hall called contending "for the legal monopoly of religious instruction, under pretence of securing the morals of the people," as "a similar kind of policy with that of the papists, who withhold the Scriptures from the common people, lest they should be betrayed into heresy."

In Hall's view, Christians of all denominations should act together "against the common adversary," but he was not prepared to support universal educational provision "if the price to be paid was a substantial extension of the establishment principle." Hall believed that the alliance between Church and State was "little more than a compact between the priest and the magistrate to betray the liberties of mankind, both civil and religious."

In his approach to millennialism, Thomas reiterated the teaching contained in an article in *The General Baptist Magazine* for July

1854. This showed no sympathy for pre-millennialism which had little appeal for most Baptists at that time, but seems to have been creeping back by the time that Thomas expressed his opinions in his first address as President of the Baptist Union in 1872. Post-millennialism fitted much better with Thomas's very moderate Calvinism and belief in the steady spread of the Gospel and the extension of Christian values by preaching and teaching and the pattern of life practised by chapel membership.

This reflects the picture that R. Tudur Jones painted of the scope of Christ's atonement being extended to all people because of the relationship between the death of Christ and the whole of mankind. As Christ's death was central and relevant to the whole of human life and the Christian had to testify to this truth in every possible way, moral, missionary, social and political, so God's tenderness and mercy provided fertile soil for the extension of the Church's mission to the whole world. More especially, responsibility for mission meant communication of the Gospel in the language of the people.

Much has been written about the strength of Nonconformity being among the working classes and Nonconformity in Wales representing *Y Werin*, the people (*Gwerin*). However, the sociology of religion has been found, after close inspection, to be less of an exact science than was once thought and later scholarship has thrown doubts on earlier work. This suggested that Baptists were generally poor people whose ministers were despised by those of other denominations, after the manner of Mark Rutherford's fictional village of Cowfold in the 1840's, where the Baptist was "a poor man", and " poor persons sat under him . . . about fifty sullen, half-stupid, wholly ignorant people."

That was far from the truth of Thomas Thomas and his con-gregation at Crane Street. Neither he nor his congregation could be described as poor, stupid or ignorant. It could be argued that he had to do two jobs to earn a living wage, and he inherited property and money through his father, but he retired to 45, The Walk, Cardiff and bequeathed to his son his personal estate of £4,572.4s. in 1881, equivalent to £500,000 in today's values. It still remained true that most Baptist churches contained large numbers of poor people and Baptist congregations were usually poorer than Congregational churches. The earlier sociological picture of Baptists being somewhere near the bottom of society with Anglicans generally near the top, has been modified by scholars in the last fifteen years. Recent studies of the geography of Victorian religion have shown that the strength and social status of different denominations varied from one region to another.

By 1851, the Baptist Chapels of Pontypool regularly received twenty-eight per cent of the population while the number of English-speaking immigrant workers in Pontypool went on increasing until more than 89% of the population of Pontypool could speak nothing but English in 1891. It is therefore very wide of the mark to claim that industrial workers were lost to the Church of England throughout Wales because the Church failed to provide services in Welsh. On the contrary, they were lost to Church and Nonconformity if there was inadequate worship in the only language that they understood.

The point needs to be emphasised because it tells us much about Thomas Thomas and industrial Monmouthshire in his time. The point has been very well made by Dai Smith in *Wales, A Question for History*. It is, as he says, never "to suggest that the Welsh language ... did not permeate the historical experience of modern Wales. It is rather to repeat that it was, nonetheless, in English that the characteristic literature, politics and social intercourse of that forming society was conducted," and no intercourse was more important than that which communicated the language of religion, and that language was increasingly less Welsh in industrial Monmouthshire as the nineteenth century progressed, and that "is not made less so by pretending that the factors involved were avoidable."

Two further areas need to be considered in assessing Thomas's character. The first involves his relationship with the Church family in Crane Street and the micro-culture of the Chapel world there.

If it is true that the Reformation was "the ultimate triumph of Augustine's doctrine of grace over Augustine's doctrine of the Church" as Benjamin B. Warfield claimed, then Crane Street failed the Reformation test and joined the ranks of the radical Reformers. The Reformers thought that the doctrine of grace was so overwhelmingly important that they could tolerate, for the sake of justification by faith alone, the divisions in the Church that Augustine deplored.

What can be made of the exclusions from Chapel membership at Crane Street, as many as 26 in less than thirty years? Some were for immoral behaviour, and that is all that the record book has to say about it. Some were excluded for dishonourable conduct or long absences, for intemperance or for being a Chartist. Fred Dauncey was excluded in 1844 for "failure in trade" when he was running a local draper's shop at the age of twenty-seven. Sixteen years later he had become a station master, but there is no record of his restoration to membership although his wife continued to attend Chapel. Deacons went out in pairs to investigate members who were under surveillance. In August 1867, "several brethren" made "serious observations" about members who were absent, especially those who "engaged in the liquor trade and kept open their houses for business on the Lord's Day." Clearly none of the deacons, all male in the time of Thomas Thomas, thought of dropping in for a drink on the way home from Chapel. Thomas was certainly not one with whom they could be light hearted about alcohol in those heady days before the Welsh Sunday Closing Act.

A more serious reason for exclusion had occurred in October 1866 when George Joshua had been put in prison for dishonesty. George seems never to have been restored to the fellowship of Crane Street, but it is to Thomas Thomas's credit that the Church heard the sermons of his son, Caleb, who trained for the ministry at Pontypool and was ordained in Desborough, Northants in 1878. Caleb's own son, Clifford became a famous New York preacher.

Thomas's personal care for the families of those who were excluded by the Church is some illustration of the working of divine grace, but the exclusions "set limits to God's liberty," to use the words of Archbishop Rowan Williams when he described Luther's opposition to the radical Reformed community because it "laid down stringent conditions of behaviour separating it from the public life around."

Perhaps the final word of assessment ought to rest in the relationship of this great Christian leader with his own family and by extension with the family of students who lived in his house at Pontypool and to whom for many years he was a father figure. Thomas and Mary faced much personal sorrow and tragedy in their lives, but they remained firm and resolute in faith and love.

The sorrows took a greater toll on Mary than they did on him and for the last twelve years of her life she was incapacitated by a severe stroke. Yet still they went on serving students for the Baptist Ministry in Pontypool. It was J. Witton Davies, a Nonconformist divine and father of a future Archdeacon of Oxford, who wrote to Thomas Henry Thomas in 1902 and described the impression left from his days as a student at Pontypool:

> "The late Dr Thomas was a man whom I loved and admired when I was a pupil in his classes and a member, so to speak of his household. Since leaving the college over which he presided—we left together in 1877—the love and admiration have grown, and I find this is the general experience of those that studied at Pontypool in your father's time. A finer type of the Christian gentleman I have never come across and very few that could be compared with him. Your mother was very much liked as you know."

The few personal letters that remain through the uncatalogued collection of Thomas Henry Thomas in three boxes in Cardiff Library, reveal a deeply affectionate Christian family, touching in their love for one another particularly in the 1850s when tragedy struck. They corresponded in English, which seems to have become the language of the home, and it was as natural for the sons to be educated in England as in Wales. William began his training for the Baptist ministry in Stepney and his mother wrote in October 1850,

> "I always thought that you would do better in Stepney or Bristol than here, put your trust in God and all will be well. We had baptising last Thursday evening. The attendance was good for a week evening. Your father is gone to Pisgah to-day to the re-opening of their Chapel. He is to preach in the afternoon."

In the same letter, Mary Thomas referred to her concern about "your dear little brother," Thomas Henry, that he also should be converted to the Christian faith. Thomas Henry, was well educated, widely travelled and became as famous in his own field as his father was in his; both his parents worried about his religious conversion.

In May 1857, when he was eighteen, his father wrote to welcome his positive attitude towards Christianity, and he went on,

> "From what you say I perceive that you feel that you are a sinner in the sight of God, though you are not conscious of that depth of conviction which has characterised the conversion of some who have gone to great lengths into open sin."

Thomas and Mary both lectured Thomas Henry about the evils of drinking and smoking. In May 1857, in the British School at Pontypool there had been,

> "two very good lectures on temperance and the liquor traffic, a strong and affecting . . . view of the physical, political and moral results of the liquor traffic and the drinking customs of society . . . which to my mind exceeds in criminality and atrocity the very slavery of the United States."

On 23 February 1864, Mary Thomas wrote to Thomas Henry on her thirty-fourth wedding anniversary. He was in Rome and she said that it gave her great pleasure to know that he was well and got to Rome in time to see the carnival, "and especially to obtain the Pope's blessing, which I hope you duly value, not that it could do you any good . . . the truths of the Gospel are too much rooted in your heart to believe in such false doctrine."

Thomas Henry was nearly twenty-five at the time. He was the only surviving child of Mary and Thomas Thomas. He was a most gifted, generous and loving son and he was with them in their last days in Cardiff. He became a pillar of Cardiff society and a major contributor to the cultural life of Wales. Whether he ever experienced the conversion for which his parents prayed is not recorded. God's time-scale is not ours but modern readers may wish that the whole Church could recapture Augustine's doctrine of the Church as well as his doctrine of Grace. It was Augustine's doctrine of Grace that inspired Martin Luther and the Reformation and brought division to the church. Augustine's doctrine of the Church was in favour of her continuing unity even at the cost of appeasing the Donatists who caused schism in the Church in fourth century Africa.

Massive integrity merging into holiness, clear vision and intelligent leadership were the gifts that Thomas Thomas brought to the tasks of his time. He had plenty of passion but not apparently as much in the pulpit as his uneducated predecessors. That was the opinion of some who "protested that, with the professionals, came the end of passion" in the pulpit, yet Russell Davies who made that observation also placed Thomas Thomas first in the list of the stars of the Nonconformist pulpit who were college trained.

In 1955, in an article to mark the one hundred and fiftieth anniversary of Thomas's birth, the Baptist historian, Mervyn Himbury, described him as "one of the most significant figures in the history of Nonconformity in South Wales," because Thomas was a pioneer in the development of the political power and social influence of Nonconformity. In the years following the second centenary of Thomas's birth, that judgement still holds true, but its truth has not been absorbed. The strength of his leadership and the initiatives that he created remain unappreciated. After his move to Pontypool to preside over the new phase in the life of the Baptist College, there was no further talk of Particular Baptists or hyper-Calvinism in his hearing.

The creation of the Monmouthshire English Baptist Association was owed chiefly to his vision as was the proposal to move the Baptist College from Pontypool to Cardiff. At a time when most Baptist Ministers rarely strayed beyond the boundaries of their own chapels, Thomas was foremost among the radicals who set up the branch of the Complete Suffrage Union in Pontypool after supporting the work of the Anti-Corn Law League. He spearheaded the Anti-State Church Association in Pontypool and its committee was active in Monmouthshire. Thomas championed the cause of the Liberation Society and he was probably the first person to realise that Wales could go it alone in seeking disestablishment. He was the first person to propose the formation of the Pontypool Church Rate Abolition Society in 1834. Thanks to him the Baptists of Monmouthshire were in the vanguard of Temperance reform. The educational voluntaryists were strongest in South Wales and Thomas was their chief apologist and ring-leader in Monmouthshire. Nefydd always put the name of Thomas Thomas first among his opponents here.

No one who reads Thomas's prose could accuse him of lacking passion. In real life, his passion was always tempered with politeness. No better example could be given of this than the acknowledgement by Jelinger Symons in his report on the state of education in Monmouthshire in 1847, that,

> "the Reverend Mr Thomas, the principal of the Baptist College at Pontypool, (he had not yet received his honorary doctorate, but his name appears first in the list as usual) . . . and other Dissenters of influence who expressed in no measured terms their disapproval of the Minutes of Council, gave me very valuable assistance in the prosecution of my labours, which I am desirous of acknowledging with thanks."

Ever true to his integrity, Thomas took the thanks and travelled to Cardiff to trounce the contents of the Report. He was a man who meant what he said and said what he meant. His students knew his worth best and that is usually a good sign. When they thought he would leave Pontypool in 1856, they presented him and his wife with their portraits in oil—and they made him stay.

When Thomas Thomas died in 1881, the cause of Welsh disestablishment had not even been formally placed on the programme of the Liberal Party. That had to wait another six years and the campaign itself would drag on for decades, until the Welsh Church Act for the disestablishment and disendowment of the Church of England in Wales was passed in time to be suspended by the 1914-1918 war. The arguments of the nonconformists in favour of disestablishment had all been well rehearsed by Thomas Thomas and the process of achievement had been prepared by him as long ago as 1862. The nonconformist disabilities, against which he fought all his life, were the subject of a book published by Dr William Edwards, his student and successor in 1912 in preparation for the disestablishment bill of 1913. It was William Edwards who also carried out another of Thomas's cherished initiatives by taking the Baptist College from Pontypool to Cardiff on 26 October 1893, as depicted by a cartoon in the *Western Mail* on that day.

The ecclesiastical reorganisation of the Diocese of Llandaff under Bishop Ollivant, 1849-1882, considerably improved the weak position in which the diocese was placed in 1850. Ollivant's first Visitation Charge in September 1851 was a far-sighted assessment of the tasks that lay ahead of the diocese. Ollivant recognised that Nonconformity had provided what the Church had failed to afford and "had it not been for the exertions of the dissenting bodies, our people must have been consigned to a practical heathenism, and left in ignorance of the name of Christ, having no hope and without God in the World."

Bishop Ollivant transformed the Diocese of Llandaff during his thirty-three years as bishop there. At the same time, Thomas

Thomas, the equally forceful and intelligent leader in Pontypool ensured that the Established Church never captured industrial South Wales from Nonconformity. His arguments are still being heard in the counsels of Wales today.

Select Bibliography

Manuscripts and Primary Printed Material

Nefydd Manuscripts, Diaries, Journal and Letters.

Manuscript 21923-4B. Texts of almost 6,000 sermons preached by Thomas Thomas, 1830-81, with details of the date, place and occasion of delivery.

Bute papers (National Library of Wales, Aberystwyth).

Publications of Thomas Thomas.

Annual Reports of Pontypool Baptist College, 1863-80 (Regent's Park College, Oxford).

Personal Letters and family papers in boxes 1.676, 4.432 and 4.433 (Cardiff City Library).

Haines Collection. Some of Thomas's publications including the Circular Letters (City of Newport Reference Library).
Thomas's Address to the Liberation Society Meeting at Swansea in 1862 (City of Swansea Library).

Crane Street Chapel Records. The Diary of Micah Thomas (Gwent Record Office, Cwmbran).

Parish Registers of Holy Baptism, Marriages and Burials for the Thomas Family in the Diocese of Llandaff. Llandaff Dean and Chapter Records (South Glamorgan Record Office).

Newspapers

Cambrian
Cardiff Times
Monmouthshire Merlin
Pontypool Free Press
South Wales Daily News

Secondary Material

T. M. Bassett, *The Welsh Baptists*; Ilston House Press, Swansea, 1977.

P. M. H. Bell, *Disestablishment in Ireland and Wales*, S.P.C.K, 1969.

Kenneth Brown, *A Social History of the Nonconformist Ministry in England and Wales, 1800-1830*, Clarendon Press, Oxford, 1988.

Roger L. Brown, *David Howell, A Pool of Spirituality*, Gee & Son, Denbigh, 1998.

Roger L. Brown, *John Griffith, The Unmitred Bishop*, Tair Eglwys Press, Welshpool, 2007.

W. L. Burn, *The Age of Equipoise*, W. W. Norton & Co., New York, 1964.

Owen Chadwick, *The Victorian Church*, 2 vols, Oxford Univ. Press, 1966 and 1970.

E. T. Davies, *Monmouthshire Schools and Education to 1870*, Starsons, Risca, 1957.

E. T. Davies, *Religion in the Industrial Revolution in South Wales*, Univ. of Wales Press, Cardiff, 1965.

Russell Davies, *Hope and Heartbreak, A Social History of Wales and the Welsh, 1776-1871*, Univ. of Wales Press, Cardiff, 2005.

A. J. Edwards, *Archbishop Green*, Gomer Press, Llandysul, 1986.

Noah Feldman, *Divided by God*, Farrar, Strauss & Giroux, New York, 2005.

Geraint Fielder, *Grace, Grit and Gumption*, Evangelical Movement of Wales, Bridgend, 2000.

D. Mervyn Himbury, *The South Wales Baptist College, 1807-1957*, Gomer Press, Llandysul, 1957.

D. Mervyn Himbury, *Thomas Thomas*, Baptist Quarterly Review XV, 1955-56.

K. Theodore Hoppen, *The Mid-Victorian Generation, 1846*-1886, Clarendon Press, Oxford, 1998.

Geraint H. Jenkins, Ed, *Language and Community in the Nineteenth Century*, Univ. of Wales Press, Cardiff, 1998.

Anthony Jones, *Welsh Chapels*, Alan Sutton Publishing, Swansea, 1996.

Brynmor Pierce Jones, *Sowing Beside All Waters, The Baptist Heritage of Gwent*, Gwent Baptist Association, Cwmbran, 1985.

David J. V. Jones, *The Last Rising*, OUP, 1985.

Ieuan Gwynedd Jones, *Explorations and Explanations*, Gomer Press, Llandysul, 1981.

Ieuan Gwynedd Jones, *Mid-Victorian Wales*, Univ. of Wales Press, Cardiff, 1992.

R. Tudur Jones, *Congregationalism in Wales* (Ed. Robert Pope), Univ. of Wales Press, Cardiff, 2004.

G. S. Kenrick, *The population of Pontypool and the Parish of Trevethin*, London, 1840.

W. R. Lambert, *Drink and Sobriety in Victorian Wales 1820*-1895, Univ of Wales Press, Cardiff, 1983.

D. Hugh Matthews, *From Abergavenny to Cardiff, History of the South Wales Baptist College, 1806*-2006, Gwasg Ilston, Abertawe, 2007.

Alister E. McGrath, *Reformation Thought*, Blackwell, Oxford, 1988.

Joseph Morgan, *A Biography of the Revd David James*, Pontypool, 1925.

Kenneth O. Morgan, *Freedom or Sacrilege? A History of the Campaign for Welsh Disestablishment*, Church in Wales, Penarth, 1965.

Kenneth O. Morgan, *Wales in British Politics, 1868*-1922, Univ. of Wales Press, Cardiff, 1970.

Thomas Morgan, *The Life and Works of the Rev. Thomas Thomas D.D.*, Carmarthen, 1925.

Vyrnwy Morgan, *Welsh Religious Leaders in the Victorian Era*, James Nisbet & Co, London, 1903.

Vyrnwy Morgan, *Welsh Political and Educational Leaders in the Victorian Era*, James Nisbet & Co, London, 1908.

Ernest A. Payne, *The Baptist Union*, The Carey Kingsgate Press, London, 1958.

Evan Powell, *History of Tredegar*, Newport, 1902.

Thomas Rees, *History of Protestant Nonconformity in Wales from its rise in 1633*, John Snow, London, 1883.

Jane Shaw & Alan Kreider (eds), *Culture and the Nonconformist Tradition*, Univ. of Wales Press, Cardiff, 1999.

Tim Shenton, *Christmas Evans*, Evangelical Press, Darlington, 2001.

Dai Smith, *A Question for History*, Seren, 1999.

Richard Hanbury Tenison, *The Hanburys of Monmouthshire*, Nat. Library of Wales, Aberystwyth, 1995.

D. J. Thomas, *A Short History of the Monmouthshire English Baptist Association*, Newport, 1957.

Ryland Wallace *Organise! Organise! Organise! A Study of Reform Agitations in Wales 1840-1886*, Univ. of Wales Press, Cardiff, 1991.

Ivor Wilks, *South Wales and the Rising of 1839*, Croom Helm, 1984.

Wilton D. Wills, The Established Church in the Diocese of Llandaff, 1850-1870, *Welsh History Review*, Vol. 4, 1969.

Wilton D. Wills, The Clergy in Society in Mid-Victorian South Wales, *Journal of the Historical Society of the Church in Wales*, 24; 1974.

Llewellyn Woodward, *The Age of Reform 1815-1870*, Oxford Univ. Press 1962.

Rowan Williams, *Why Study the Past?* DLT, 2005.

Glossary of Theological Terms

Arminianism

Arminius himself was a Dutch Reformed theologian (1560-1609). He denounced the deterministic logic of Calvinism by which people were predestined before birth to eternal salvation or eternal damnation. He denied that Divine Sovereignty was incompatible with real free will. He taught that Jesus Christ died for all people and not just for the elect. In England and Wales the term Arminian described the anti-Calvinistic trend of Anglican theology in the seventeenth century and the Wesleyan Methodists in the eighteenth century.

Calvinism

Calvinism derives from the teachings of the French Reformer and theologian, John Calvin (1509-64). Central to Calvinism is the doctrine of the Absolute Sovereignty of God. The basis of all Christian faith is the Word of God revealed in the Holy Scriptures. Human beings cannot win salvation except through the free grace of God. Human free-will is denied after the fall of Adam and even before the fall for some Calvinists. The absolute predestination to eternal life or eternal damnation was later rejected by moderate Calvinists.

Particular (Strict) and General Baptists

Baptists, more correctly Anabaptists, because they believed in adult believer's baptism and rejected the baptism of infants, were first found in England as a congregation in London in 1612. Their theology was Arminian and they were General Baptists. A congregation of London separatists whose theology was Calvinist became a church of Particular Baptists in London in 1633. The first Baptist church in Wales was founded at Ilston on Gower in 1649. General Baptists had an Arminian view of salvation and gave a prominent place to associations of local churches. The theology of Particular Baptists was Calvinist.

Pelagianism

This takes its name from teaching formulated by Pelagius, a British monk at the beginning of the fifth century. Pelagius taught that human salvation was achieved by human efforts without the assistance of free grace. Pelagianism was condemned by St Augustine.

Arianism

This is derived from the teachings of Arius, a priest at Alexandria at the beginning of the fourth century. Arius denied that Jesus is the divine Son of God but regarded him as a creation of the Father. The teaching of Arius was refuted by Athanasius and condemned at the Council of Nicea in 325.

Socinianism

This term was used for those who followed anti-Trinitarian teaching which denied the divinity of Christ and resulted in Unitarian doctrines that were merely deistic. The name Socinian derived from two Italians, natives of Siena in the sixteenth century.

Fullerism

This represented the teachings of Andrew Fuller, Baptist Minister at Soham in 1775 and at Kettering in 1782 until his death in 1815. In his book *The Gospel worthy of all Acceptance*, he condemned hyper-Calvinism. He believed in the universality of the Atonement and human free-will. His views were influential in England, Wales and America.

Sandemanianism

This represented the teaching of Robert Sandeman (1718-71), the son-in-law of John Glas (1695-1773) from whom Sandeman derived most of his teaching. They were both Scotsmen. They both wanted the complete separation of Church and State. Sandeman treated faith as if it were bare intellectual belief without feeling. His views were strongly denounced by Andrew Fuller who taught that faith involved the whole person. Baptists in North Wales suffered from the coldness of spirit and lack of prayer that characterised Sandemanianism at the end of the eighteenth century.

Appendix

List of Publications by Thomas Thomas, 1835–1877

Letter dated May 8, 1857 from Thomas Thomas to his son,
Thomas Henry Thomas

Letter dated February 23, 1864 from Mary Thomas to her son,
Thomas Henry Thomas

Extract from the Annual Report 1877
of the Baptist Theological Institution, Pontypool

The Conway Family Tree

LIST OF PUBLICATIONS BY THOMAS THOMAS, 1835–1877

1. Pastoral Letter addressed to the Church of Christ meeting at Henrietta Street Chapel; 25 November 1835.

2. The Civil Duties of Christians: a sermon occasioned by the late outrages at Newport, Monmouthshire, preached at the English Chapel, Trosnant, Pontypool by Thomas Thomas; London 1839.

3. A Proper consideration of the Cause of the Poor, a test of righteous character. A discourse designed to advance the object of the Manchester Conference; Pontypool, 12 September 1841; London 1841.

4. The Duty of Religious Men to study the times in which they live and to apply their energies to the right conduct of public affairs; Pontypool, 9 November 1847; Newport, 10 November 1847. The first of seven lectures on the present duties devolving on Christian professors as members of a civil community; London 1847.

5. The Christian Duty of Determined Adherence to right principles; Pontypool, 21 December 1847; Newport 23 December 1847 (Lecture 7); London 1847.

6. The Duties of Christian Citizens, Circular Letter to the Monmouthshire Baptist Association meetings; Sirhowy, 25 and 26 May 1847; Cardiff 1847.

7. The importance of developing the Power of Welsh Nonconformity for the Liberation of Religion from State Patronage and Control. Paper read at the Conference of the Liberation Society; Swansea, 23 and 24 September, 1862; London 1862.

8. The things that are most surely believed among us. Circular Letter of the Monmouthshire English Baptist Association; Cardiff 1866.

9. The Inaugural Address of the Revd Dr Thomas at the Annual Session of the Baptist Union; London, 22 April 1872.

10. Baptists and Christian Union. The address of the Revd Thomas Thomas D.D., Chairman of the Baptist Union of Great Britain and Ireland; Manchester 10 and 11 October 1872.

11. Memoirs of the Life and Labours of the Revd Thomas Jones of Chepstow including an autobiography, edited by the Revd Thomas Thomas D.D., President of Pontypool College; London 1875.

12. The Leaven of the Modern Pharisees and Sadducees. Circular Letter of the Monmouthshire English Baptist Association; Cardiff 1877.

SELECTION OF PERSONAL LETTERS

1. Letter from Thomas Thomas to Thomas Henry Thomas

seen what next day reach'd
us, she would have discover'd
a gleam of hopeful &
cheering light amidst the
gloom & Darkness

From what you say I perceive
that you feel that you are
a sinner in the sight of God,
tho' you are not conscious of
that depth of conviction which
has characterized the conversion
of some who have run great
lengths into open sin. It is
rather what I have observed in the
majority of young persons who
have had a religious education
& what I have myself felt
the gentle drawings of God's
Spirit by means of the word
& the dispensations of Providence
I hope you will continue to feel
them still more strongly till
you cheerfully submit to the yoke
of the Savior's authority. "Draw

me, & we will run after thee. It is well to set up for ourselves a high standard of religious excellence & labour constantly to attain to it — or rather to accept that perfect standard wh God has given us in his word & in the example of his Son. But we do wrong if we suffer our own conscious imperfections, or the shortcomings of professors to deter us from a decided & open profession of the gospel. I have known several cases — & now know several — of persons whose religious character is hopeful, but who deprive themselves of much true consolation & greatly restrict their usefulness from a consciousness of their own defects & a perception of the disparity ~~of~~ between their Conduct & professed views & the law of Xt. Such feelings ought to produce a different result — an immediate practical effort to approximate to the standard of duty by openly keeping the commands of Jesus, & looking up from time to the perfect

Exemplar! I hope & pray you may be enabled to do so. For this purpose make prayer a habit, & the Bible your companion & guide amidst eager professional pursuits. And if you could attend the devotional meetings of the week & settle down at one place, I think you will find it advantageous in several respects.

On the point of pledged temperance, I do not wish to impose any thing on your own conviction. Do approve. I have no faith whatever in the physical benefits of any of the strong drinks used in our country, & the moral dangers are palpable & obvious to all on the surface of society. And therefore I cannot but wish you & all my dear ones & friends to abstain. A pledge if the result of conviction is an additional security amidst the snares of both worlds & so called religious society & also an open testimony against the usages of our country. Should I learn that matters to the decision of your own mind, assured you will do what

Note: This letter ends above the beginning of the letter

2. Letter from Mary Thomas to Thomas Henry Thomas

Baptist College
Feb. 23/64

My dear T Henry

Your last letter
gave us great pleasure. especially to know that you were
well and happy. We had been
for days expecting to hear fr you.
especially your poor Mother
before your letter arrived. I hope
you will not think me neglect
about you because I have not
written before, but be assured
that I take a lively interest
in all your movements and
that of your young companion.
You say but little about him
I hope you find him a pleasant and

an interesting companion.
When are we to expect you
home? it seems a long time
since you left. I am glad
that you got to Rome
in time to see the Carnival
and especially to obtain the
Pope's blessing, which I
hope you duely value.
not that it could do you
any good. I flatter myself
that the truths of the
Gospel are too much
rooted in your heart to
believe in such false doctrine
I hope my dear child that
you do not forget to commune

with you
that your conduct is such as
becometh the gospel of Jesus Christ
My prayer is that you may
be kept from all sin.
Since you left I have had
some sickness and your dear father
has been very poorly also. I never
remember him so ill before
but God in mercy has restored
him to health again.
Mrs Evans of (Delhi) has been
with us for some time and
has been very poorly eversince
she has been here which has
given me some trouble and
anxiety, but she is better and
will leave next Friday I hope.
I have not any particular news
to give you. Pontypool is much

the same as when you left
except that Death has carried
away some that you knew. Mrs
Shellow and Rebecka Richards
the blind girls sister that
used to sit in chapel behind
our pew. Have you had your
likeness taken since you left
if not get one and send it
me, that I may have some
idea what sort of a face you
have now. I must leave a little
space for your father to say a word
or two to you. So with much love
I remain your affectionate Mother
Mary Thomas

You ought to have found 2 letters from me
at the Rome P. Office. You seem to refer to only
one. Your last was a fortnight coming, & we had
begun to feel a little anxious. You will, no
doubt, visit the Catacombs with the other wonders
of the Eternal City. Are its "Seven hills" now
distinguishable & prominent? I shall be glad
if you will bring me a good map of Rome, My father
you can get one pretty cheap. T. Thos.

Note: **Thomas Thomas's postscript on his wife's letter**

EXTRACT FROM ANNUAL REPORT 1877 OF THE
BAPTIST THEOLOGICAL INSTITUTION, PONTYPOOL

THE REPORTS OF THE TUTORS.

THEOLOGY.

REV. T. THOMAS, D.D.

In this department the *Senior Class* produced Ten Essays on the *Holy Scriptures*, comprising the Canon of the New Testament; the Genuineness of the Sacred Writings, their Authenticity, and their Plenary Inspiration; and the Apocryphal Books of the Old and New Testament.

The *Junior Class* went through a lengthened course of study on the History of the Kingdom of Israel from the Revolt to the Asyrian Captivity; also, the History of the Kingdom of Judah to the Babyloniah Captivity; the Restoration of the Jews; the rebuilding of the Temple, and the re-establishment of Divine Worship, and the Administration of Ezra and Nehemiah, with notices of the great Miracles and Revelations of those times. This Class also attended *Twenty-six Lectures* on the United Kingdom of Israel, during the reigns of Saul, David, and Solomon.

The two Classes alike composed Essays and received Lectures on the chief questions relating to the *Christian Church*, comprising its Constitution, its supreme Head, the Character of its Members, its Rights, & Duties: The Apostles, Prophets, and Evangelists as its Extraordinary and Temporary Officers; Pastors and Deacons as its ordinary and permanent Officers; its Ordinances, Baptism, and the Lord's Supper; the Means of its support and Extension, as divinely appointed and sufficient in opposition to Ecclesiastical Establishments; and the most prevalent errors relating to the Church and its Ordinances. The Seniors, however, proceeded to the study of the teaching of the Word with regard to Christian Assemblies, the Lord's Day, and the Service of Prayer and Praise.

Twenty-five Sermons were read by Students in rotation for criticism by the Tutors and the young men.

PONTYPOOL, *May 23rd*, 1877.

" To the Committee of the Pontypool Baptist College.

"Gentlemen,—I beg to submit to you the report on the examination of the Students in Divinity this year. They had, as divided into two classes, pursued a course of study on the Constitution of the Christian Church, its Officers, Ordinances, Support, Government, &c. and what we hold to be errors prevailing on these important points. A paper was prepared for each class containing questions, not only on the above course, but also on points connected with it, which have been brought into prominence in recent times, by the romanizing clergy of the National Church. I am very pleased to state that the gentlemen dealt with the papers in the most satisfactory manner. Not one paper approached a failure. Most of the replies were marked by intelligence, pointedness, and accuracy; the work of one or two of the Students is entitled to even higher praise than this. I scarcely need therefore say that the result of this examination reflects well upon the ability and diligence of the Students, and adds its tribute of honour to those of preceding years to the successful tuition of the "Master in Israel," who for so many years has filled the Theological chair, and who by his long and distinguished service to the College, has made it 'a praise in all the Churches.'

"Earnestly hoping that Dr. and Mrs. Thomas may be spared to enjoy their well-earned rest and honours, and that the College, under its new President, may flourish in continued efficiency and prosperity.

"I am, Gentlemen, yours truly,

"E. D. WILKS."

DIVINITY.

SENIOR CLASS.—Joseph Davies, 95; John Meredith, 90; W. J. Price, 89; D. B. Richards, 88; J. J. Hughes, 87; John Rees, 80; E. E. Probert, 76; John Edwards, 74; J. E. Jones, 62; J. A. James, 60.

THE CONWAY FAMILY TREE

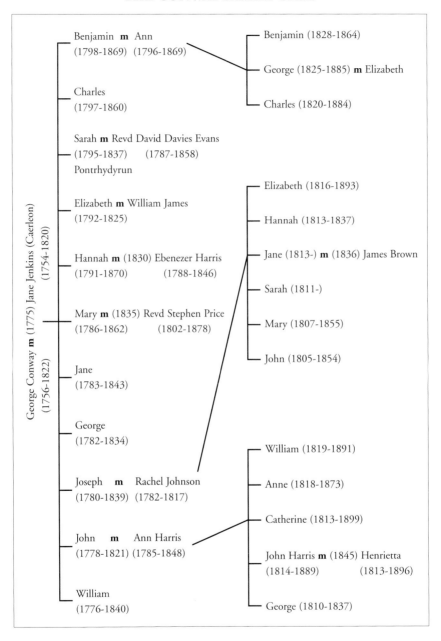

Index of People and Places